# TESTIMONIALS

Peter has a heart for service and courageously seeking excellence. He's been through a divorce and raised a lovely, grounded, amazing daughter, Alie, by practicing harmony and compassion throughout the years with his ex-wife.

– Angie Monko, transformational life coach

Peter Hobler is a rare blend of value in business and relationship wisdom. Not from theory or interviewing others, but through his own personal experiences. As an author: exceptional! As a speaker: most valuable! As a coach: edifying! Whatever and whoever he comes into contact with will be forever changed for the better.

– Viliami "Coach V" Tuivai, *Life Champion* success coach, keynote speaker, and author

I met Peter after losing my father. Peter has had a significant influence in my personal life and for my personal family dynamics. His heartfelt attention, guidance, and insights have deeply impacted my own personal development leading to my having more self-confidence and a more insightful understanding for how to be self-empowered in all areas of my life. Thanks to Peter, my marriage and my approach to fatherhood have completely changed in ways I never knew possible.

– Jordan Zabel, project manager

At one of the most challenging points in my life, Peter helped me "dig deep" to rediscover my strength, ability, and belief in myself to transform my life into what I envisioned. He is an outstanding coach who cares deeply about his clients and effectively facilitates the mindset and practices of success!

– L. Ashton, PhD, president/CEO of Evaluation Enterprises, LLC

Peter Hobler has a passion for empowering people to move past their subconscious fears to realize their fullest potential, and a gift for bringing out their very best from within through his practical teachings. His remarkable talent has been refined from years of "walking the walk" and teaching from real-world experience.
– JT DeBolt, mission accomplishment expert

Peter Hobler has been a mentor, a coach, and a visionary who exemplifies the highest qualities of integrity, compassion, and friendship. I am extremely grateful for his insight, guidance, and support. Peter has a masterful knack for knowing when to bring out clarity of purpose and desire that is often hard to pinpoint on your own.
– Dr. Chris Heeb, CEO, St. Louis BEMER Group

When I met Peter, I was living my personal definition of hell. I felt stuck in a cycle of seemingly non-optional decisions born of trauma and fear. I searched for my exit route: drugs, food, frivolousness, books, and attempted suicide. Eventually I Googled a question, hoping for an answer for how to escape my misery—and I found Peter. His coaching helped me to feel valued, empowered, and free. He gave me a gift of gratitude that changed the trajectory of, and even saved, my life. My wish for anyone who craves more from life, regardless of their situation, is that they get to experience the leadership, service, and insight Peter can provide.
– Kaelei M. Johnson, real estate specialist and beauty consultant

Divorce and differences of opinion do not have to derail good parenting, and Peter's book *Split Harmony: Turn The Ex-Factor from Chaos to Compassion* encourages co-parenting in many positive ways.
– Judy L. Rubin, Partner, Plaza Advisory Group, Inc.

# SPLIT HARMONY

*Turn the "Ex-Factor" from Chaos to Compassion*

PETER HOBLER

UNION SQUARE
PUBLISHING

Published by
Union Square Publishing
301 E. 57th Street, 4th floor
New York, NY 10022
www.unionsquarepublishing.com

Copyright © 2018 by Peter Hobler

All rights reserved. No part of this book may be reproduced or transmitted in any form or by in any means, electronic or mechanical, including photocopying, recording, or by any information storage and retrieval system, without the written permission of the Publisher, except where permitted by law.

Manufactured in the United States of America, or in the United Kingdom when distributed elsewhere.

Hobler, Peter
    Split Harmony: Turn The "Ex-Factor" from Chaos to Compassion
    LCCN: 2018946462
    ISBN: 978-1-946928-18-4
    eBook: 978-1-946928-19-1

Cover design: Joe Potter
Copyediting: Claudia Volkman
Interior design: Claudia Volkman
Photo credits: David McCarthy/www.davidmccarthyphotography.com

www.theex-factor.com

## DEDICATION

To my daughter, Alie:

I love you with all my heart and soul, now and forever. I am grateful for the joy you bring to me and to everyone in your life. I am joyful for the gratitude you have for life. I hope and pray you learn a fraction as much from me as I have learned and continue to learn from you. My love is always with you, wherever you are. Spread your wings and soar far and high my beloved Alie Girl.

All my love, Dad

# GRATEFUL ACKNOWLEDGMENTS

I'd like to express my gratitude for the individuals who have supported me in making *Split Harmony* an inspiring and impactful reality.

I give my heartfelt thanks to the people who have had the most profound impact and influence on me as a parent and in my life. These inspiring individuals have provided meaningful insights and support for me during extraordinarily difficult and challenging times.

Pastor Gretchen Pickeral, thank you for being there in the beginning. When I was first separated, things seemed hopeless. In you I found that special someone to talk with, to listen to me, and to ask me hard, reflective questions.

Dr. Dean Allen, thanks to you and your program, *The BodyTalk System*, I gleaned incredible and meaningful insights about my innermost *subconscious fears* and how to become *aware* when they were in control of my decision-making processes. Your teachings, insights, questions, homework assignments, and accountability ignited the spark that led to the underlying premise of this very book. Thank you for this dramatic, life-shifting awakening, Dean.

Dr. Rand Olson, thank you for being a consistent supporter, sounding board, wise sage, and friend for more than fourteen years. Your ability to listen, ask provocative questions requiring in-depth inner reflection (on my part), your insight, and your energy for life have led to a huge shift for me to develop more *awareness* and start taking personal *responsibility* for my words, choices, and actions.

To JT DeBolt, my first personal success coach, your passionate commitment and ability to listen, comprehend, and challenge me by asking tough questions helped me expand my mental and spiritual capacity. You are an inspiring mentor and true friend.

Rene Kamstra entered my life in 2012 when she became my

personal coach. Rene's intuition, insights, knowledge, *awareness*, and unconditional friendship have had a profound impact on my life.

Leisa Jenkins's specialty is coaching coaches. Leisa, know that I deeply appreciate you and your commitment to your own self-growth and to those whose lives you touch, in this case my daughter's, my family's, my own, my inner circle of friends', and the other special people in my life.

I would be utterly remiss if I did not thank my parents, individually and together, for their unconditional love, for always being there, and for the lessons I've learned the hard way.

Thank you from my heart to Laurie Zabrowski, an absolutely incredible woman who recently entered my life. Laurie, I am grateful and proud to call you my best friend, confidante, fiancée, and life partner. Thank you for your insights and especially for your support. Laurie, I love you with all my heart. I am excited and committed to our future together.

Most of all, I want to express my immense, heartfelt gratitude to my daughter. Alie, you have grown into an amazingly *aware*, insightful, and inspiring young lady. You are wise, charismatic, charming, poised beyond your years, caring, grateful, and a good judge of character. As I've shared with your mother numerous times, in spite of the two of us, we must have done something right! I love you with all my grateful heart forever and beyond.

Thank you to the team at Union Square Publishing: Rick Frishman, Scott Frishman, and Karen Strauss. Thank you to my editors, Cheryl Ross and Claudia Volkman, and to my cover and design specialist, Joe Potter. And a thank you for insights and suggestions from members of the Quantum Leap team, especially Martha Bullen and Deb Englander.

Rick, Scott, and Karen, your expertise, insights, passion, and care for the *Split Harmony* project have been a blessing on all fronts. Know I consider each and all of you a part of my family.

I am grateful for my book architect, Justin Spizman, who shared empowering insights and feedback to transform *Split Harmony* into a significantly more inspiring and powerful book. Justin, you are my kindred spirit in this project. Know that I already consider you a dear friend. Thank you.

# CONTENTS

## Section I: *COURAGE*, the Story, and the Lessons

Introduction: *Split Harmony* Takes *COURAGE* ...............................3
Chapter 1: A Whirlwind Romance.................................................7
Chapter 2: The Downward Spiral................................................13
Chapter 3: Lessons Learned (the Hard Way)................................21
Chapter 4: The Underlying Cause...............................................27
Chapter 5: The *Vicious Cycle of Subconscious Fear*......................37

## Section II: The Impact (of Your Behavior) on Your Kids

Chapter 6: When Kids Shut Down or Overreact..........................47
Chapter 7: Emotional Distress....................................................59
Chapter 8: Emotional Abandonment..........................................73
Chapter 9: The Pitfalls of Parental Competition..........................79
Chapter 10: The Example You Set as a Parent.............................87
Chapter 11: Consciously Choose the Seeds You Plant..................93

## Section III: Nurturing *Split Harmony*

Chapter 12: Step 1: *Forgiveness*..................................................101
Chapter 13: Step 2: *Clarity* of Destination: What Do You Really Want to Create for Your Children?............................................107

Chapter 14: Step 3: *Awareness*: Where It All Begins ................113
Chapter 15: Step 4: The *Ripple Effect of Awareness*......................119
Chapter 16: Step 5: Taking Personal *Responsibility*.....................127

## Section IV: Making *Split Harmony* a Reality

Chapter 17: The Benefits of Compromise...................................137
Chapter 18: Be Your Best Self No Matter What!.......................145
Chapter 19: Creating and Nurturing *Split Harmony: Forgiveness + Clarity + Awareness + Responsibility = Split Harmony*..................155
Postlude: Four Steps to Begin Nurturing *Split Harmony*...............161
About the Author ....................................................................162

## SECTION I

## *COURAGE,* THE STORY, AND THE LESSONS

It requires *COURAGE* to create a shift in the ways you "naturally" react to and deal with the communications and interactions of your relationships, particularly with your ex or ex-to-be. I share the most significant aspects of my personal story so you can relate and better grasp the concepts and lessons in *Split Harmony*.

# INTRODUCTION

## *SPLIT HARMONY* TAKES *COURAGE*

I wrote this book for the benefit of the precious children of divorce. Through sharing insights, guidance, and lessons to inspire parents to become more *aware*, I am confident they can better control their angst-charged reactions and transform their behavior. My family's process, and the one I will share with you, included *forgiveness* and the *COURAGE* principles of *clarity of destination*, *awareness*, and *responsibility*.

*Split harmony* can be created when parents of separation and divorce realize their anxiety-fueled, reactive behavior sets a poor example for their kids. When you step into the realm of taking personal *responsibility*, your heightened *awareness* of the impact your words and behavior are having on your children will help you set a positive, life-changing example. This shift creates a more nurturing emotional and psychological environment for your children

If you are one of the majority of parents going through divorce who are in a high-energy, reactive, two-way accusatory, fearful, and unbelievably stressful scenario, understand that it takes heartfelt commitment to be open-minded, to listen, and to begin working on yourself. This is what is required to take your children out of the middle of the harrowing situation between you and your ex or ex-to-be. (Throughout the rest of *Split Harmony*, whenever "ex" is used it refers to your ex or ex-to-be).

To provide a consistently nurturing environment for their children, parents of divorce must have *COURAGE* to let go of angst and lack of trust. Why *COURAGE*? Because it takes *COURAGE* to recognize that your words, choices, actions, behavior, and the resulting consequences all set examples for your children. Because it takes *COURAGE* to let go of your fear-fueled anger so you can step up and be the best parent you can be, to compromise, to work together, to start taking personal *responsibility* for your words, choices, actions, and the effects on your children.

For the sake of your children, commit to the intention to foster the concepts in this book. A beneficial side effect is less stress for the entire former family unit. I know because my ex-wife and I created *split harmony* for our entire former family for the sake of our now adult daughter, Alie.

It is vital to know what you really want for your children. Without having *clarity* for what this is, you'll very likely end up creating something completely different, especially when you are focused on what you don't want!

Once you know what you want for your kids, ask yourself if your behavior is aligned with these goals. If you are angry and reactive, blaming your ex, or stuck in your fear, know that you are not nurturing what you want for your children. More than likely you are teaching them the opposite through the example of your own reactive behavior. Shifting your perspective away from self-centeredness to the mutual priority of your children while navigating the murky waters of divorce begins to create a shift of focus. This different energy cultivates distinctly more integrity-based core values for your children.

*Split Harmony* provides the foundation for this shift by sharing insights, guidance, lessons, epiphanies, and experiences to help you realize how dissipating trust leads to fear-based reactivity, which is harmful for your children, for yourself, and for all family members.

## INTRODUCTION

Remember, it takes courage to put down the proverbial "boxing gloves" for the benefit of your children.

In *Split Harmony*, we will focus on four foundational principles:

1. *Forgiveness*
2. *Clarity of Destination*
3. *Awareness*
4. *Responsibility*

In the forthcoming pages, we will discuss each of these in much greater depth.

The *Vicious Cycle of Subconscious Fear* is the driving force behind reactivity. From my experience and observations, this reactionary behavior exhibits an outpouring of anguish and accusations, the undercurrent of which often stirs up devastating emotional waves, especially for your children.

As you reflect on a possible lack of *awareness* about the consequences of your reactive-fueled words and actions, take a deep, slow, calming breath. Realize there is always room for personal growth and for the self-transformation it takes to plant seeds that will nurture *split harmony*. This takes humility, a rare characteristic in the world today.

As a parent of divorce, when you are willing to see what your anger is doing, you can start to listen and strive to do your part to work together as a parenting team. This could be as basic as a mutual commitment to STOP reacting to each other. This will be one of the most incredible and positive gifts you will ever give to your children, to yourself, and to your entire family. And if the other parent refuses, at least you are doing your part to make things better for your kids and for yourself. Stress is detrimental to health, happiness, joy, and inner peace—for anyone and everyone.

Though this book is for all parents of divorce, *Split Harmony* also aims to specifically provide enlightenment for dedicated dads of divorce. Men typically do not want to ask for help. They do not want to admit they are afraid to be open and vulnerable. Men tend to think vulnerability is being weak. The reality: *Being vulnerable* requires calm inner confidence and true *strength of character*.

Let go of the egotistical part of you that is keeping you from being openhearted and vulnerable. The gifts to you and your children will be enormous and absolutely life-shifting. One of the biggest gifts you can give your kids is to stop planting seeds of emotional trauma via your reactive behavior.

As a parent, it's time to step up and commit to having heightened *awareness* and take personal *responsibility* for your choices, actions, or reactions, and for the consequences of each that follow. As you can imagine, this is a vital aspect of success in any realm of life.

*Split Harmony* is for you if you are committed to being the best parent you can be and believe you are up to following through with the self-discipline and self-work necessary to take your kids *"out of the middle"* of the separation and divorce scenario.

God bless your children. Godspeed to you and to all parents. May your children realize that you consistently and consciously have their best interests in your mind and heart. Understand the difference this will make in their lives, now and for the future.

# CHAPTER 1

## A WHIRLWIND ROMANCE

The beginning of my relationship with my ex-wife makes for a wonderful and adventurous love story filled with romance, passion, excitement, and mutual anticipation of things to come.

I was with a group of seven friends on a fun-packed ski trip to Keystone, Colorado, in February 1990. After an exhilarating, speed-filled, thrilling day on the slopes, we were reveling in après ski activities at the base of the mountain. Out of the blue, I heard someone yell "Peter!" from across the bar. It was Bill, a friend of mine from back home—a small-world coincidence for sure! We excitedly hugged and agreed to meet for dinner that night.

Bill knew three girls from home who were also in Keystone and invited them to join us. We had an awesome evening filled with good food, fun, and laughter. Little did I know that one of the three friends, Kathy, would soon become my wife.

We arranged to ski as a group the next day at Copper Mountain. The three girls arrived late. However, we managed to connect and skied together the rest of the day, laughing, whooping, hollering, and trying to show off for each other.

After the Wild West trip, I called Kathy every once in a while to say hello. I didn't ask her out, however, because I was dating someone else. That relationship ended about two months later. Soon afterward, I asked Kathy out, and on May 5 we went on our first date, a black-tie function. Dressed in my tux, I picked up Kathy, and we headed to the Ritz-Carlton.

As each couple entered the fund-raiser, a photographer snapped their picture. Ours would prove to be one of the best pictures ever taken of the two of us. We had a wonderful time during this special evening. It was filled with philanthropy, drinks, dinner, lots of conversation, smiles and laughs, and some dancing. The romantic adventure had just begun.

Ten weeks after our first date, I proposed during a special and creative evening of romance, dinner, and flowers. My proposal was set to a song my brother had written for the occasion. After dinner, a 1936 Rolls-Royce Phantom limousine took us to Metropolitan Square, the tallest building in St. Louis.

Once there, we took an elevator straight to the unfinished top floor (thanks to a friend with connections). We walked around sipping Dom Perignon in wonderment as we gazed out at the myriad of brilliant, twinkling lights of the cities of St. Louis, Missouri and East St. Louis, Illinois.

What a whirlwind romance we had leading up to our engagement and wedding! A little more than six months after our first date, we were married on November 24. Not long after, we decided we wanted to expand our family. After trying to get pregnant for a year, we spoke to a fertility expert and had some testing done. The results suggested we needed help. After two rounds of insemination attempts, the doctor recommended we go to the next level: in vitro fertilization.

This proved to be an extremely stressful experience, particularly for Kathy. Today, I believe any couple considering fertility treatments should speak with a relationship counselor beforehand. It's important to understand the challenges of hormonal and emotional imbalances that can potentially result from infertility and fertility procedures.

If we had been informed of the ways this process could impact our relationship, we could have had the foresight to learn how to stop subconsciously reacting with anger or frustration when things didn't go "our way" or got out of control. This realization led me to understand that during interactions with anyone, I can choose to remain calm by not allowing my trigger "buttons" to be pushed. This has been a truly life-changing epiphany.

While we were struggling to get pregnant, things took a further nosedive. We became *aware* that we did not know each other very well. Had anger taken over? It seemed as though we didn't want to make an honest attempt to resolve things between us. We no longer had honest, open communication to express our innermost thoughts and feelings. With the built-up emotional frustration and simmering anger, the trust we had nurtured dissipated, and we began to lose our faith in each other and possibly in ourselves. It seemed that I couldn't say or do anything right. I imagine this was the same for Kathy.

In spite of the heightened challenges and resulting stress, and thanks to in-vitro fertility efforts, we did finally get pregnant. We were both completely off-the-charts excited. Nine months later, our special Alie Girl came into the world.

The day of Alie's birth was one of the most joyful days of my life. It was a miraculous moment—a special, happy day. Just after Alie was born, she cried like a little banshee. I walked over to her, put my head next to hers, and started singing a song I had made up about the moon and seeing Alie soon. I used to sing it to her every night before she was born with my head on her mother's stomach. As soon as she heard me singing her song, she was quiet immediately and turned her head toward me.

We had a lot of fun choosing a name. We never figured out a name for a boy, but narrowed it down to two if we had a girl: Alexandria and Alexandra. We decided Alexandria was too preppie for the mountains of Jackson Hole (where we visited regularly), so we chose Alexandra.

The new responsibilities, interactions, and additional stresses of parenting and trying to work together for the sake of our daughter took a toll on us in many ways. We managed to make it through another two years. Disagreements, arguments, and accusations were a part of our everyday life.

I started to withdraw and shut down. We each became increasingly sensitive and reactive to even the most mundane situations. We blamed each other. Neither one of us took any real personal *responsibility* for our words, choices, actions, or the resulting consequences. We lived in a fear-fueled, emotionally reactive battleground.

A mind-blowing five-week trip to southern France ended up being the last adventure of our marriage. For a month, we rented a phenomenal three-hundred-year-old stone farmhouse with a swimming pool outside of St. Rémy-de-Provence. We started the trip with three days in Paris. Then we took a bullet train south to our final destination just outside of St. Rémy.

It was an incredible five weeks. We alternated spending days at the farmhouse and exploring in our leased silver Peugeot. We relaxed at the farmhouse, typically hanging out by the pool and popping into St. Rémy to go to the farmers market to buy delectably fresh French culinary items such as paté, cheese, vegetables, fruit, and homemade delicacies.

On the days we ventured out, we'd drive to the surrounding regions and towns of Provence: Châteauneuf-du-Pape, Arles, Avignon, Aix-en-Provence, and more. We saw jaw-dropping historic ruins, enjoyed palate-teasing and pleasing lunches at little country restaurants, passed beautiful fields filled with huge, yellow, bursting-with-sunshine poppies, experienced the running of the bulls in St. Rémy, and drove some of the most beautiful country roads imaginable. We were so fortunate to experience such an amazing and memorable trip.

However, the entire time in France, a tightwire-type tension filled the air between us. I was excited to feel like we were finally having some connection toward the end of our trip. Reflecting back, I remember thinking that our relationship was in a reconciliation mode.

In the beginning we shared love, excitement, passion, and anticipation for wonderful things to come for our future life together. The process of trying to have children definitely took its toll on us. In hindsight, I've wondered if it would have been possible for me to be less reactive or even nonreactive to make things less volatile between the two of us. I remember that there were so many wonderful, exciting, and happy aspects about having a child. There were also additional emotional and psychological challenges, something we had never discussed with each other or likely ever thought about individually. Foresight can be such a gift.

When Alie was born, being new parents was such a wonderful, happy time. However, within a few years the downward spiral started, and I found myself wondering, *What happened?*

It is difficult to say just how our behavior as parents affected and impacted our daughter during the challenges of our marriage and even more since our divorce. Certainly there had to be tremendous emotional confusion for our then-three-year-old during the initial times of our separation and divorce.

Since our divorce, our behavior jointly and separately has undoubtedly had the greatest psychological impact on Alie. This includes the ways we shifted to set more positive examples and the ways we unknowingly conditioned and planted seeds of *subconscious fear* in our child via our reactive words and behavior.

Developing heightened *awareness* for how your behavior affects your children will help you be more conscious with your words and behavior. This is a blessing that is truly in your kids' best interests.

# CHAPTER 2

## THE DOWNWARD SPIRAL

A few days after we returned home from southern France, Kathy asked me to move out of the house. I was shocked and disappointed, but I moved out immediately. Even then, I don't think either one of us realized the end was in sight. We were reacting to our darkest fears, being disrespectful and, suffice it to say, "not nice" to each other. We were on an out-of-control downward spiral, a ride that had led us to this point of no return.

Unfortunately, as seems to happen in so many separation/divorce scenarios, our trust in each other plummeted. We were constantly afraid we'd try to take advantage of each other, which made us feel like we were walking on eggshells. I was afraid Kathy would try to keep me from being with Alie. Kathy was afraid she would not get any financial support. Our communications continued to break down, and what remained of our relationship went into a final tailspin from which we never recovered.

Our marriage came to an end in several ways. The emotional "love" had dwindled and faded away. During the time leading up to and after our separation, our trust waned and constant frustration and reactive anger, which were so detrimental to our daughter, replaced it.

Our divorce wasn't pleasant, but it could have been much worse. After it was finalized, we were no longer committed to each other. We had one mutual goal: to have at least enough *awareness* to provide a more balanced environment for our daughter.

The bond of love and trust that once brought us together ended before we divorced. Today, because of our mutual desire and commitment to make our daughter our number one priority, we now trust each other in the realm of parenting our treasured child. While we still do not always agree, we can almost always communicate in a calm manner and figure things out.

Listening is one of the most important aspects of any parenting relationship, and we each strive to improve in this realm. Reactive anger still occurs on occasion, especially when any aspect of finances and money come up.

So, when and where did things go wrong?

Looking back, we never shared true, expressive, openhearted communication. As a result, we did not know each other very well. Probably we did not even know ourselves.

This took its toll, especially during the challenging fertility process. This mutually reactive experience changed our perceptions of each other for the worst.

Since our divorce, there have certainly been bumps in the road, most of which we have worked through, though occasionally the frustration has been so great that we have gone months without speaking. I hope we will continue to work on raising our respective levels of *awareness* so we can continue to put our differences aside and figure out ways to compromise, make more empowering choices, and work together on Alie's behalf.

Without having *clarity, awareness,* and *responsibility,* the conditioned tendency is to react from *subconscious fear,* which, over time, will sabotage almost any relationship.

The absolute most unfortunate aspect of our situation was that

## THE DOWNWARD SPIRAL

we were each, separately and together, putting our beloved daughter, Alie, *in the middle* via our reactive words and behavior. When you hear that "*awareness* is where it all begins," in the realm of divorce, this is even more paramount. It takes *awareness* and effort on both "sides" to create *split harmony* for children of divorce and for the entire former family unit.

It is impossible to change anyone else. Understanding this, I knew I could only work on changing myself. I started to focus on being the best dad I could be for my special Alie Girl. This included being *aware* and striving to keep her *out of the middle* between her mom and me. Creating an environment of *split harmony* requires consistently following through on being your best, on striving to be accepting, calm, and proactive (*not* reactive). This certainly includes not taking your ex's reactiveness or anger personally.

I also realize I cannot change anything that has already happened. However, I can change how and what I think about past difficult experiences. With this in mind, I've made the conscious choice to learn and grow from life's challenges. With this new "state of mind," I have become more *aware* and subsequently have more introspective, reflective, and insightful observations about the ways my ex and I tended to explosively react to situations and to each other.

Most people know what they do NOT want, and this is what they focus on. I believe this is one of the biggest reasons disharmony arises in the majority of divorces. When you are afraid of what the other person will do, you subconsciously end up walking on eggshells, which puts forth a very negative and resistant energy. Gaining *clarity* for what you want dramatically shifts this energy.

As I developed *awareness* from this insight, I also gained *clarity* about the ways I do NOT want to handle things in any given situation. So I can now consciously shift my focus to what I really DO want and how I need to intentionally BE to create what I want, especially for Alie.

From the moment Alie was born, she has been the single most important part of my life. She has brought endless joy and love into my life. I feel so blessed and grateful. To this day, I continue to learn more from her than she may ever learn from me.

Alie's mom and I agreed to try to find a professional counselor to help us communicate. Over the last few years of our married relationship, my ex-wife and I met with five or six marriage counselors and attended regular weekly counseling sessions. Every time a counselor suggested that Kathy needed to change (at least her behavior) or questioned her in a way she didn't like, she would mandate that we find a new counselor. Eventually she refused to continue further counseling.

One of the single most important realizations of my life is that you can learn significant lessons as a direct result of going through the most difficult and challenging situations. Of course, you must personally choose to put down the boxing gloves and intentionally look for the opportunity to learn and grow.

Being a parent, with the responsibilities and challenges that come with having children, is one of life's greatest privileges. I have shifted my perspective on our rocky road of separation and divorce and am now grateful for the abundant lessons I've learned, often the hard way. These lessons are what I strive to share with you in this book.

When once loving, blissful marriages take a turn south and head toward divorce, the majority of couples seem to end up completely closing off all open, honest, and vulnerable communication with each other. One or both refuse to talk to the other, and there ends up being a lot of resentment and resistance. I believe this is often the result of lost faith and trust in one another. This is such a tragic and unnecessary side effect of divorce.

As a parent, you need to put your children first. This means being committed to communicating and working on having faith and trust in each other *as parents* for the sake of your children. It means no tit-for-tat retaliation for each other's anger-fueled, reactive behavior. Choose to be calm and rational, not reactive. You can decide to not allow your buttons to be pushed.

Consistently making decisions for the right reasons—that is, what is best for your children—involves taking the high road. When both parents can mutually commit to do this, it directly benefits not only your children, but both of you as well.

This sets a profoundly better example for your kids. As they grow up, they will have a more deeply seated positive emotional and psychological foundation because they will have innately learned about the *awareness* it takes to make self-empowering decisions in their own life situations and relationships.

When one or both parents are subconsciously self-focused and self-centered, they tend to be overly protective in very reactionary ways. This often vindictive behavior begins to mold the very same underlying dynamics within the psyche of the children. Is this something you want for your children? Of course not.

Constantly reacting to each other with anger and making accusations not only further destroys the trust the two of you once had, it negatively impacts your children by putting them directly *in the middle* of the ongoing battleground the two of you have created. And yes, it is vital to step up and recognize **your** personal *responsibility*. Blaming the other parent is the opposite of taking *responsibility* and tends to lead to brawl after brawl. This consistently puts your children *in the middle*.

To serve the best interests of the whole family, as a parent it is important to remain calm, levelheaded, and to work on having a heightened level of conscious *awareness* to make sure your children are truly your number one priority, and ultimately the mutually agreed-upon top priority for you and your ex.

Reflecting on the outcome of our divorce experience, *split harmony* is a very real possibility. Our daughter is living proof of the resulting positive influence and impact of the shifts created through *forgiveness*, gaining *clarity* for what we wanted for our daughter, working on having heightened *awareness*, and stepping into taking personal *responsibility* for our respective choices. I am beyond proud to introduce Alie to anyone, anywhere, and anytime.

My ex-wife is good friends with my sister and my mom to this day. At first, this was pretty challenging for me. Once I realized it wasn't about me, I stopped taking things personally and put Alie first. I was able to shift my perspective and be accepting of the relationships between my ex and my family.

As a parent, each and every one of your words, actions, and reactions sets an example for and affects your children. This may have an immediate impact, planting potentially damaging emotional and psychological seeds that could grow into stifling *subconscious fears*. As a parent, why would you consciously want to do this?

Think about the huge positive difference it will make when you strive to develop heightened *awareness* to shift your behavior and the subsequent outcomes and consequences for your children and for yourself. Whether you realize it or not, in many ways your example plays a vital role in forming the foundational conditioning for the integrity and character of your children.

You may think you are doing an excellent job of parenting, yet the harsh reality is that often you are teaching your kids to be overly controlling, selfish, paranoid, materialistic, quick to react with anger, and on the list goes.

Doesn't it make more sense to intentionally strive to be *aware* and consistently BE and do your best to make your children the top priority, especially during the duress of separation and divorce?

When you have *clarity* regarding what you want for your children, you can learn to stop your reactive, anguished behavior and set a more empowering example for them. This includes having the goal to remain calm no matter what. (Yes, over time this does become easier).

## THE DOWNWARD SPIRAL

An important reflective question I asked myself was, *Why would I want to do anything other than help my ex-spouse be the best parent she can be for our daughter?* I wanted my ex to be the best mom she could be. I realized this included my support. And I wanted the same from her so I could be the best possible dad. After I stopped letting my ex push my buttons, I realized I was no longer giving her fuel to get pissed off at me. Think about this: When you get angry at someone, don't they typically get angry right back at you?

Yes, at times this has been extremely challenging due to anger-based reactions from my ex-wife (and times when I likewise have made it difficult for her). We both love our daughter unconditionally. After all, doesn't it make more sense to work together than against each other as parents of divorce?

# CHAPTER 3

## LESSONS LEARNED (THE HARD WAY)

Life's challenges offer the most impactful opportunities to learn and grow. The experience of separation and divorce certainly brings many of these challenges to the forefront. You can learn some of the most valuable life lessons from the personal experiences and interactions with your ex or ex-to-be.

People are conditioned to focus on what they do NOT want. Every time you realize you are focused on what you do not want, use it as an *awareness trigger* to hone in on what you DO want. This will help you to stop, think, and act instead of unknowingly reacting to *subconscious fears* with frustration, anger, or blame. You can learn to use hindsight as a tool to recognize the times you tend to react with anger or disrespect. Be *aware* of your behavior and expect to be treated the same way in return. Strive to treat others the way you want to be treated, no matter the situation—yes, especially with your ex. Remember, it's worth remaining calm and under control for the sake of your children.

In regard to my behavior with my ex-wife, I learned how vitally important it is to maintain *awareness* and *responsibility* to stay calm because this is in the best interest of my daughter. Even when Alie is not present, saying something critical about her mom still puts out a negative energy. It is always better to focus on remaining calm in order not to succumb to the temptation to explode with anger, accuse, blame, or shame.

*Split Harmony* is all about sharing insights, stories, and experiences to inspire you to open your heart and eyes and to ignite your *awareness* by inspiring you to BE more *aware* of the growth opportunities behind every challenge. Simplistically put, this boils down to shifting your perspective.

Let me explain by sharing a story I recently heard during a sermon at church. The pastor, Bill, was speaking about a video he saw on Facebook. Someone bumped into a man as he was walking with a very hot cup of coffee, and the man spilled his drink. His immediate inclination was to be upset at the person who had walked into him. Before reacting from his underlying frustration at having someone spill his coffee, he asked himself, *Why did the coffee spill?*

His first judgmental answer: *Someone hadn't been paying attention and bumped into me.* He realized he was blaming the other person.

Then the real reason vividly popped into his head. The coffee had spilled because there was coffee in the cup. This made him think about what was inside of him and how he had almost allowed his frustration to spill out onto the person who had bumped into him. Suddenly he understood that there was so much goodness inside of him, and no matter what happened, his benevolence was what he wanted to spill out and share with others.

Even when something unpleasant happens, you can choose what "spills out." You can choose to react or to stay calm and continue to be the best version of yourself, the person you were when you and your future wife or husband met and began to get to know each other.

Why would you ever allow your inner fears or darkness to take over your subconscious reactions just because you find yourself in the emotional disarray leading up to or after divorce?

Reflect on what difference it would make if the two of you shared the ultimate goal of striving to work together to consistently make decisions in the best interests of your children. A major irony: this is almost always in your own best interest.

And yes, at times this can be extremely challenging. One of the myriad of personal examples was when my ex decided to buy Alie a car without talking with me. Initially I was pretty upset because I disagreed with how she had handled the situation. Once I shifted my perspective, I became grateful for the fact that she could afford to buy Alie a car. I also happily realized that I would not have to drive Alie everywhere or figure out when she would want to use my car. I also learned that I do not want to do things this same way. Instead, I would want to reach out and communicate to Kathy or at least share my plans in advance. To me this falls under the realm of respect and is the way I want to be treated in return.

Whether happily married, headed to divorce, or divorced, realize that you cannot control how the other parent chooses to "operate"— you cannot control the choices they make. Idealistically, both parents must set the best possible example for their children. But when just one parent commits to be in control of his or her fear-based emotions, it has a tremendously positive impact on the entire former family unit.

When you absolutely and resolutely commit to consistently work on your own *awareness*, you can begin to perpetually BE your best, most authentic self. This means being present so you can make choices from your heart instead of reacting to any inner turmoil, that frustration you feel when the two of you are butting heads or accusing each other. Parenting by divorced parents should and can be a team effort, and there is much greater potential for a profoundly positive impact on your children.

During the chaos of divorce, parents must mutually work on having heightened *awareness* and following through by taking personal *responsibility* to remain calm and nonreactive. You must put your differences aside and endeavor to work together synergistically in the realm of parenting—again for the emotional and psychological well-being of your kids.

For the benefit of your children, reflect on whether you personally want to strive to be aligned with or antagonistic toward your ex or ex-to-be. Contemplate which choice will have positive ramifications for your kids and which will cause potentially lifelong emotional and psychological damage.

When parents refuse to work together, things can quickly turn into an out-of-control downward spiral. The only individuals who benefit from this tailspin are lawyers. The more you and your ex fight, the more money it costs, and the more you fill the pockets of the divorce attorneys. To top this off, there is less left for your children (if indeed you have decided to give them anything) or that the two of you could share or give to a worthwhile cause.

With the combination of the poor example the two of you set for your kids and the financial drain and loss over time, you are creating a monstrous type of legacy, one I think no one would want to emulate. Why are so many divorced couples so damn slow to learn from the mistakes others have made before them? Could part of it be that, like so many parents of divorce, you are listening to your naysaying friends who slam your ex and tell you not to trust him or her? Hmm ... Let me ask you again, "What do you really want for your children?" Understand that when one parent commits to be their best and nonreactive, it helps take your children out of the middle and sets a much better example for them. Inhale slowly, deeply, and then exhale deliberately. Letting go of your anger may seem next to impossible because it has so consumed you, but hopefully not so much when you really think about the benefits of letting go of it for your kids—and for yourself.

For years, I have said that communication is 10 percent what you say and 90 percent how you say it. You can express your frustration and anger while remaining calm. Following through on this creates quite a shift. By changing your own behavior, the other person will not be getting the reaction they expect, and over time they will tend to subconsciously shift their own behavior.

As parents, it is vital to realize that we set the most significant examples for our children, more so than teachers, care providers, friends, extended family members, or anyone else. When you think about this, why would you allow yourself to set the example of being combatively accusatory and distrusting with your children's other parent? When you realize what kind of example you do NOT want to set for them, you can gain *clarity* for what you DO want for your kids and strive to set the example this requires.

As kids grow up, they can choose how they want to approach and deal with situations themselves. They may do it like their mother, their father, or in their own unique way. When you set an example of *awareness* and personal *responsibility*, your children will pick up on this, and it will serve them in empowering ways for their future.

That is the ultimate goal of this book: to give you the tools, resources, and a systematic and easy-to-follow process to manifest *split harmony* within the home and during the difficult and tumultuous times that often arise when a family decides to separate. You have no greater *responsibility* than that of a parent, and this book will help you live up to that tremendous expectation.

# CHAPTER 4

## THE UNDERLYING CAUSE

Why do we react so automatically most of the time without even thinking? Typically an underlying *subconscious fear has been triggered*. An ex or ex-to-be says or does something that sets off an innermost fear, and before we know it, we're spewing an unconscious retaliatory comment, a tit-for-tat accusation, or a defensive reaction or threat.

Reflecting on my own experiences and the insights gleaned from working with mentors and personal coaches, I began to realize the impact *subconscious fear* was having on my reactive choices and behavior leading up to and after our divorce. I now understand that my fears were much more in control of my "choices," and I've been blown away by how powerful my *subconscious fear* has been throughout my life. Initially during our divorce situation, my ex-wife and I both reacted to our *subconscious fears*, and our extreme reactionary behavior severely impacted our daughter.

You must begin to recognize that what you focus on is what you get more of in return. When you are unknowingly focused on your fear, you put out energy that is resistant to attracting what you really want—if indeed you have *clarity* for what you want in the first place. This realization allows you to shift your focus, which creates a shift for what you attract in return.

For the most part, your deepest fear was very likely foundationally formed through traumatic childhood experiences, often from interactions with your parents or possibly a significant child caregiver. The resulting emotional and psychological pain endured can lead to deeply embedded, disempowering core beliefs. These create your underlying *belief system*. My favorite acronym for *belief system* comes from life coach Angie Monko, one of my dear friends. When your *belief system* is deeply rooted in fears leading to disempowering choices, Angie calls it your *BS*. How absolutely appropriate!

When I started to understand that deep-rooted fears affect the choices we make, I realized how important it was to first forgive myself and then my father, who had often corrected and reprimanded me and therefore had the greatest impact on my *belief system* (definitely my BS).

Why *forgiveness*? Because this is the first step to letting go of your angst. *Forgiveness* empowers you to shift your perspective and mindset so you can start to be your best, most authentic self. When you can be calm and stop reacting to your *BS*, it is a huge gift, especially to yourself and your children.

During my divorce, my greatest *subconscious fear* was that my ex would try to undermine my relationship with my daughter and try to "take her away from me," at least on an emotional level. I believe my ex's biggest fear was that she would not receive financial consideration.

When a profound fear is triggered, it often leads to other fears. In extreme divorce situations, parents will often try to alienate their children from their ex or ex-to-be. This is one of the most emotionally and psychologically damaging situations any parent can create for their kids. Subconsciously, children want to love both of their parents. When they are not "allowed" to love a parent, the internal trauma begins and can turn into a stifling, lifelong subconscious obstacle that can affect a child's future relationships on all levels.

## THE UNDERLYING CAUSE

Another side effect of fear: you believe that your children could end up being materialistic, self-centered, unaware, and void of good, solid listening skills due to the poor example being set by your ex. You may also be worried that your ex's "brainwashing" of your children will not teach them how to compromise, talk things through calmly, or know how to work with others.

During and after divorce, when parents are continuously reacting to each other, they are teaching their kids via the example they are setting. If you want to instill self-confidence and independence in your kids for their future relationships, you must stop and ask yourself two questions: 1) *What do I really want to teach my children?* and 2) *Am I setting an example for my kids that will teach them the things I want them to learn or the opposite?* You must be completely honest with yourself.

Reactive behavior will teach your kids to play the same type of mind games that you and your ex are into and even make them afraid to express their true thoughts and feelings in calm, confident ways. They may well end up being oblivious that they are reacting to their own *subconscious fears* as this is the example the two of you have been setting for them.

Strive to be *aware* of the circumstantial triggers that subconsciously ignite your fear, typically something someone says or does. Triggers tend to be more hypersensitive in situations with the people you are closest to because your "guard" is down.

Why? The *Vicious Cycle of Subconscious Fear* is the key. As a result of emotional pain you suffered as a child and in prior relationships—like so many people have experienced—you may have been unknowingly conditioned to feel insecure. This conditioning will have instilled fear-based core values deep within your psyche.

For me, this started with my father always correcting me and at times punishing me for things I did not do. As a result, I developed an inability to express my thoughts or feelings, even when there was no substantive evidence that I might be "screwing up." This lack of self-worth led to complete self-doubt, which in turn led to me being very shy for the first few decades of my life.

Have there ever been times during your divorce scenario that you've left a message for one of your young children on their mom's or dad's voicemail and did not hear back from them?

This happened regularly to me before Alie had her own cell phone (around age thirteen). I would jump to the conclusion that my ex was being disrespectful by not having Alie call me back. Unknowingly I allowed this to reinforce my fear that I would not be allowed to have the opportunity to nurture a loving, trust-based, open, two-way communication-based relationship with Alie, which I wanted more than anything in the world. I now realize this was Kathy's reactive behavior because of her own *subconscious fear* that I was trying to intrude on her special time with Alie.

Taking things personally will almost always trigger your *subconscious fear*. It is vital to focus on having heightened *awareness* so you do not take things personally and end up reacting negatively.

Regarding interactions with your ex, your reactiveness may be a result of your expecting negative, reactive behavior from him or her (and all too often you probably have not been disappointed). Reflect on whether it is ironic that the energy you typically emanate is focused on expecting these negative reactions. The *Law of Attraction* is all about attracting what you put out, beginning with your thoughts, words, actions, or reactions. During and after my divorce, I felt that my ex was constantly criticizing me. It seemed that everything I said was "wrong" and nothing I did was ever "good enough." Can you relate?

When you learn to view criticism as feedback, you can choose how you interpret it. An empowering choice: strive to learn and grow from any and all opinions or "assessments" from your ex. When you learn to stop taking the criticism from your ex personally, it will

## THE UNDERLYING CAUSE

help you to remain calm and stop reacting. After all, you most likely do not have a clue about what the underlying facets of her or his *belief system* are that were conditioned in childhood and reinforced in prior relationships.

For me, as I began to reflect on how often I took the reactions of my ex personally, I realized that I had always subconsciously jumped to the conclusion that I was being criticized. Being more consciously *aware* has directly helped me to be less reactive and also helped me to plant more positively nurturing seeds in my subconscious for all of my relationships. When you start viewing criticism as feedback about yourself or about the other person, it becomes much easier to maintain self-control and stay calm.

One of the most self-empowering things you can do is to check your subconscious reactions when you realize you've let people and/or circumstances trip your fear triggers—stop, think, and reflect on what actually triggered your fears. When you start to understand what triggers you, you will get a better idea of what your fears are, where they come from, and why they have been so easily triggered. This makes it easier to intentionally be more consciously *aware* so you can remain in control of yourself and your interaction in any and every circumstance.

It is absolutely essential to strive to maintain an elevated level of *awareness*. When I feel emotionally or energetically drained or am about to react with anger (due to my fears being triggered), I literally know that I do NOT want to feel this way; I know that I want to shift. In this moment, I envision a little red flag popping out of the top of my head to warn me that it's immediately time to be more consciously *aware*. I call this an *awareness trigger* . . . it's time for heightened *awareness*. I reflect on and determine how I want to feel and subsequently begin to create shifts in my thoughts and choices in that moment to make this my inner reality.

Using some form of personal *awareness triggers,* in any given moment you can make a different, more conscious choice to think things through, and then act accordingly. This directly leads to responding in a more positive fashion, which shifts the outcome for the benefit of your children and all involved.

A life-transforming realization: other people do not set you off; rather you allow your buttons to be pushed when your *subconscious fears* are in control. The underlying fear make you react in abrupt, irrational, and often abrasive ways. It is up to you and only you to decide to stop reacting and start remaining calm and in control in all situations.

Accepting and letting go of fears may be one of your most challenging undertakings, yet this is an extremely rewarding and life-changing transformation, especially for the sake of your children during and after your divorce.

Thinking back to your childhood, are there ways your mother or father handled situations with you that you did not, and still do not, like? Another aspect of heightened *awareness* is being able to recognize when you are subconsciously dealing with your children in the same ways your parents dealt with you. For me, this was a huge aha moment, one that allowed me to break this generational cycle from my childhood and positively modify my parenting technique.

A personal example: I realized I was continually correcting my daughter and telling her there was a better way to do something or say something . . . my way. Now I call a big *BS* on myself as I understand it's much more important to nurture Alie's independence than to try to force her to do things "my way," which was precisely what my dad did to me every single day. I realized that repeating this habitual behavior would serve to create a feeling of resistance and even resentment within Alie. Subsequently, I committed to achieve having enough *awareness* to dramatically shift my behavior.

I initiated a discussion with Alie and explained to her that I realized I corrected her a lot. I told her I wanted to change this

## THE UNDERLYING CAUSE

but needed her help. I'll never forget Alie's response: "Dad, are you serious?" I replied, "Yes, I am." She said, "Good luck with that, Dad!" She told me she would really like me to change my habit. Her response told me she knew I corrected her a lot and that she didn't think it would be easy for me to change this habit. Sadly, she had become used to it—what a huge aha moment for me! I came to realize I had the tendency to constantly correct Alie, just like my dad had done with me. This epiphany horrified me, and I became committed to changing this completely subconscious habit.

This episode made me realize how important it is to always allow Alie to be herself. This in turn helps her build her self-confidence, the very thing I would be taking away from her otherwise.

This is merely one example of how I recognized I'd been repeating the "parenting habits" of my own mother and father, which were having the opposite impact and effect of my actual intentions and desires for Alie, the same way as my parents had impacted me.

Admitting your oversights, downfalls, and failures is not easy. With a perspective shift, this becomes a foundational starting point to setting a better example to instill the core values that form, shape, and nurture the underlying characteristics, morals, *awareness*, and future strengths of your children.

As a parent, you are always setting examples for your kids, whether consciously or as a subconscious consequence directly stemming from your reactiveness to your ex/ex-to-be. This is one of the most vital epiphanies you can have as a parent.

As it did for me, I hope this hits you right between the eyes! Each and every time you react to your ex out of anger or frustration, not only do you lose control of yourself and the interaction, but he or she will never want to do what you want them to do, and you are putting your children *in the middle*. Putting your children *in the middle* has negative ramifications for them whether they are present or not. When you react with frustration or anger to your ex, the tendency is for her or him to be triggered and react in turn. This additional repercussive negative "energy" further entrenches your kids *in the middle*.

Developing the *awareness* it takes to remain calm and to maintain self-control may at first appear to be a lofty goal. With practice, this becomes consistently easier, smoother, and less energetically draining (for everyone).

Whenever you react with anger, you are giving your ex (or anyone for that matter) an excuse and the opportunity to immediately lose their temper and self-control. When you lose control, you end up setting it up to be this way.

This only serves to perpetuate the *Vicious Cycle of Subconscious Fear* (explained in Chapter 5), and the resulting reactive behavior from both "sides" often leads to your respective fears turning into reality, over and over again.

When you lose control, not only are you setting a terrible example for your children, you set up a losing scenario for the entire former family unit, meaning you have "lost" even more. When you get angry, the other person will not want to do what you want him or her to do. The same holds true when someone reacts with anger at you. You will never want to do whatever it is she or he wants you to do. Never.

So why is it that most parents of divorce consistently do just this? His reaction pitted against her reaction . . . her reaction leads to his reaction . . . and so the seemingly never-ending cycle goes. This is such a sad irony for your kids and for both of you, and for every reactive parent (whether divorced or not).

An ultimate personal goal is to maintain self-control, especially when it comes to interacting with your ex. When you cannot do this (for whatever reason), forgive yourself, take personal *responsibility* for your actions, take a big breath, and apologize to your ex and to your children (once they are old enough). Now you can return to integrity with yourself and with your ex/ex-to-be. Strive to reflect

## THE UNDERLYING CAUSE

on the times you end up losing control in order to continually learn from your mistakes so you can move forward in a more positive and empowering fashion, particularly for the sake of your children.

When Kathy loses her temper and goes off on me, I strive to maintain my composure. Once in a while, I lose it in return, which only serves to make the situation worse. When the heated interaction is over, I take a few big breaths, ask God for strength and composure to remain calm, and then I silently forgive Kathy from my heart. After all, her reactionary behavior is not personal. It is about her reacting to her own deeply embedded fear. This process further empowers me to get back to my committed baseline of calmness and composure.

Do you or your ex tend to want to always be right? If your answer is yes, ask yourself why this matters so much to you. Try the above process: Breathe, ask for strength and composure, and then silently forgive your ex. Yes, this takes compassion, desire, and *COURAGE*. It also takes a big heart and resolute commitment to BE your best. Being your best, most authentic self is always worth the "effort."

The key is to recognize when you are reacting, or about to react, to your ex/ex-to-be as a result of the anger being triggered from your *subconscious fears* or *dragons*. "Dragons" implies that your *subconscious fear* is a "*drag on*" your potential. They keep you from being your best, and in reality are leading to your being your worst. Is this what you want to teach your kids?

The consequences of losing control will never benefit your children or anyone else. This realization hopefully will inspire you to use your brewing anger as an *awareness trigger* (a warning sign) that losing self-control and spewing dagger-edged anger is NOT how you want to BE. Now you can focus on how you DO want to BE. With practice and repetition, this will dramatically support your ability to maintain self-composure.

Though this may be a hard pill to swallow, you and only you can transform your heretofore conditioned behavior, thereby potentially changing the outcome of almost every single interaction with your ex.

I remember the day I decided to no longer let my ex-wife push my buttons. I simply committed to remaining calm no matter what. Overall, I have consistently maintained my composure. Over time, this shift in my behavior has reconditioned the overall reactive/interactive relationship between my ex and me. The most positive impact has been and will continue to be on our daughter, Alie, the biggest *WHY* for both of us to put forth the effort in the first place.

When you decide to no longer let your ex/ex-to-be trigger you and can start to remain calm during all of your interactions, especially when he or she is purposely trying to trigger you, they will no longer be getting the reactive response they have come to expect. Over time, the inclination is for there to be a change in their behavior. I hope this makes sense to you. In a nutshell, you cannot change someone else (especially your ex). When you change your behavior, the other person will subconsciously start to shift his or her own behavior.

When you consistently apply this to your divorce scenario and life, you will be able to reflect back and feel how extremely rewarding it is to know you were able (and can still) maintain self-control in any potentially inflammatory situation with your ex—and subsequently with anyone.

How you interact with any person or situation, including your ex/ex-to-be, is up to you and only you. You can subconsciously choose to allow her or him to push your buttons and explode with anger, or you can consciously decide to maintain your composure and remain calm, directly having more positive impact on the outcome and consequences.

# CHAPTER 5

# THE *VICIOUS CYCLE OF SUBCONSCIOUS FEAR*

*Subconscious fear* is a topic that keeps popping up yet is something few people take the time to comprehend. What you focus on is what you get more of in return. When you subconsciously focus on your fear, you not only put out resistance to what you really want, but end up attracting people, situations, and things connected to your fear, which tends to make your fears come to fruition. When you focus on your fear, the energy you emanate has the propensity to make your fear come true. This is why I call it the *Vicious Cycle of Subconscious Fear*.

So, just what is *subconscious fear*? *Subconscious fear* stems from painful childhood experiences that create the foundational aspect of your underlying core *belief system*. The huge unfortunate aspect of this *belief system* is that it ends up revolving around fear. A great acronym for *belief system*, as I mentioned previously, is *BS*.

*Subconscious fear* is the greatest barrier to your success. For example, when you were a child, your parents' behavior, words, disciplinary action (or lack thereof), ability to communicate (or not), all instilled deeply embedded *subconscious* conditioning in you. A lot of this conditioning likely resulted from some form of emotional pain. This pain in turn planted seeds of *subconscious fear* that subsequently formed your *core beliefs*. These *core beliefs* continue to affect how you think and react to this day. As you continue to make choices that are unknowingly based on your fears, you put out an energy that attracts more of the same. This also puts out resistance to what you really want, if indeed you've put in the time and effort to gain *clarity* for what you really want. As a parent, this includes knowing what you want to create for your kids via your own behavior.

Over the years, I have invested a lot of time reading, talking with professional counselors, coaches, and mentors, as well as journaling, reflecting, and studying the topics of *subconscious fear* and *awareness*. As a result, I have become more *aware* of my *subconscious fear* and how I once unknowingly allowed it to keep me from being the person I was born to be.

By doing so, I focused on developing the *awareness* it takes to make more conscious choices, especially in those moments and interactions where I had the tendency to react with frustration or anger. The outcome of this effort has directly and dramatically impacted my life and my daughter's in extremely positive ways. A bonus side effect has been its unmistakable impact on the entire former family unit, including my relationship with my ex-wife. As I mentioned earlier in the book, she continues to participate in activities with my side of the family when it benefits our daughter, Alie.

This might sound crazy to you. It's definitely not the norm. But when it comes to all the nasty divorce scenarios, who would want to be like everyone else? So here's a question for you: Do you think my ex and I were able to reduce the emotional stress factor and set a more positive example for our daughter?

Absolutely yes! Considerable beneficial effects occur when you break the "normal" way of going through divorce. The results are less stress, less strife, less chaos, and even less financial drain (money going to the divorce attorneys), more compassion, and overall better health. Most importantly, there is much less emotional and psychological trauma for your children.

# THE *VICIOUS CYCLE OF SUBCONSCIOUS FEAR*

Progress for you (and for any parent going through the challenges and duress of divorce) will be a direct result of your personal commitment and efforts for self-processing, inner reflection, self-work, and the resulting self-growth that leads to life-changing shifts for the sake of your children.

Every challenging experience in life can be turned into an opportunity to learn and grow. This may seem impossible, but it is a conscious choice, one that you can learn to consistently make.

The most vital aspect of *subconscious fear* is to break out of it by developing enhanced *awareness* about how your reactive behavior and decision making directly impact the lives of your children.

In the realm of divorce (and life in general), most individuals are unaware of their tendency to subconsciously *react* to situations with anger, fear, or frustration. When you begin to think through situations rationally and make conscious choices about how you interact and deal with the people and circumstances you find to be the most difficult, the consequences will lead to more positive outcomes for your kids.

When you find yourself suddenly getting angry or frustrated and then blame the other person, what is it that sets you off? When you absolutely commit to work on increasing your self-*awareness*, you may begin to realize your anger and frustration are subconscious reactions stemming from *subconscious fears*.

Now you can develop the aptitude to leave your reactive behavior behind. When you have *clarity* for what you really want for your kids and start to focus on being the person it takes to create it for them, your children—and you—will experience a dramatic and desirable shift in the environment of divorce.

Imagine you suddenly find yourself in an argument with your ex regarding a school activity, such as a play or a sporting event. Sounds familiar already, you say?

How did the argument start? Maybe you said something the

other parent didn't like and they reacted with anger, or there was a disagreement about who was taking the kids to the event.

Your ex/ex-to-be gets angry, and their reactive anger sets you off. The two of you proceed to engage in verbal warfare. Each of you are now consumed with incensed anger toward one another.

Have you ever stopped to think about the effects your black, reactive-fueled emotions have on your children? Or how the stress is negatively impacting your own health?

Perhaps the other parent exploded, and you ended up completely shutting down all modes of interpersonal communication, leaving an invisible, simmering shroud of anger rooted inside of you. Your anger completely paralyzed your conscious thought-processing ability, and without giving it a second thought, you turned and walked away (leaving nothing resolved).

A life-shifting thought process and realization for life's future encounters and interactions is that you cannot change circumstances, things, or other people. Period. However, you can change *your* behavior when you develop the *awareness* to consciously choose *how* you want to intentionally *BE* when you find yourself in reactionary scenarios. Changing *your* behavior can lead to amazingly positive results, including reducing your own stress and over time decreasing the explosive reactionary behavior from your ex (since they are no longer receiving the expected reactions in return from you). Over time, you begin to shift the outcome of what happens next.

Insightful questions to ask yourself when you lose your self-control are: *Why did I lose my temper?* and *What subconscious fear triggered my anger?*

When you start to take personal *responsibility* for your words, choices, actions, reactions, and your overall behavior and can honestly and objectively answer these questions, you will start to have more objective inner reflections and figure out how to maintain your composure. More importantly, you can create a calmer, less stressful

## THE *VICIOUS CYCLE OF SUBCONSCIOUS FEAR*

environment, leading to a more highly positive-emanating energy that has a much more favorable impact on your children.

When you react with anger, do you think you get what is best for you or for your children? Do you think your ex will ever want to do what you want him or her to do when you are yelling at them? Do you ever want to do what he or she wants you to do when they are yelling at you?

Are you *aware* of the times you've put your children *in the middle*, either directly or indirectly? Have you blamed your ex/ex-to-be, or have you taken personal *responsibility* when you've put your kids *in the middle*?

Have your actions resulted in the other parent wanting to work with you toward a common goal for how to raise your children in a harmonious environment? If not, then it's time to look in the mirror and think about your role and how it's contributed to the inflammatory situation you and your ex find yourselves in. This may be a hard pill to swallow, but blaming your ex will not change a thing. Rather, it will continue to be a *trigger* for her/him leading to more dissension and controversy between the two of you. This is wickedly detrimental to your children and to your own serenity, health, stress levels, and well-being.

### Make the Shift

Shifting your perspective is a learned approach to help you think about how you would ultimately act (that's right, act, *not* react) in a situation with the other parent when neither of you is angry at the other. Why would you want to do try this? Because you will be more likely to keep your composure and remain calm, which means you have learned the art of restraint.

Make this concept a real goal and consciously practice applying it in every interaction, especially when anger or frustration are trying to raise their ugly heads.

Remember, by transforming how you interact with the other parent, he/she may eventually change their behavior because they will no longer be getting the reactions from you they have come to expect.

I don't know about you, but I do NOT feel good about myself after I've exploded at someone with anger, even when it's my ex-wife!

Anger is a major barrier to mutually figuring out what is best for your children. The bottom line: You have lost self-control when you allow your fears to rule your decision-making processes. As a result, the best-case scenario for your children will most likely not occur. When you are constantly reacting to your fears and lashing out, the family ends up in turmoil and chaos.

Breaking the *Vicious Cycle of Subconscious Fear* may seem to be daunting and challenging, but it is one of the greatest gifts you can ever give to your children and to yourself.

### • Reflective Questions •

*Write down your responses and thoughts for the greatest insight. Do the work, experience the growth, and create* split harmony.

- What are your biggest *subconscious fears*?
- What triggers these fears—that is, what causes you to react to them?
- If you could figure out how to stop reacting to your fears, how would this impact your relationships and your life?
- How did having children affect your relationship with your spouse?
- How has your behavior affected your children? (Reflect openly and honestly.)
- How has the trust between you and your spouse been affected by your divorce?

## THE *VICIOUS CYCLE OF SUBCONSCIOUS FEAR*

- Do you blame your ex for the challenges between the two of you, or do you take personal *responsibility* for **your** words, choices, actions, reactions, and the resulting consequences?
- Do you believe the two of you have the potential to work together amicably in the best interests of your children?
- Why or why not?
- As a parent, you are always teaching your kids through your behavior. What do you believe you are teaching your children from the ways you interact with your ex/ex-to-be?

# SECTION II

# THE IMPACT (OF YOUR BEHAVIOR) ON YOUR KIDS

As a parent, your behavior impacts your children. What you say and do—whether you are calm and rational or upset and unreasonable—teaches your children similar core values they will use throughout their lives.

The all-too-often extreme angst that seems to accompany divorce subconsciously conditions your children for their future and their relationships.

It's so very important to have *Clarity* for what you want to create for your children and to ask yourself if your words, behavior, and choices are going to lead to this outcome. This section will help you better understand how your actions and choices impact your children's deep emotions and feelings. Then, we will work to shift your approach to grow into the parent you've always wanted to be.

# CHAPTER 6

## WHEN KIDS SHUT DOWN OR OVERREACT

Up to this point, we have gone back in time and reflected on how you were conditioned in childhood, and how at the beginning of your marriage there was love, romance, and excitement. We then shifted to discuss how dramatically things changed, leading up to the present scenario between you and your ex/ex-to-be. The challenges of life, particularly in the experiences of separation and divorce, can lead to lessons learned, most often the hard way. Typically, tremendously heightened angst exists between former spouses, and it leads to hair-triggered reactiveness. The underlying cause of this is almost always *subconscious fear*. When you glean *clarity* for what you want for your kids, you can ask yourself if your behavior is creating this for them.

As a parent, you must understand that children learn from the behavior of the individuals in their immediate environment—first and foremost parents, and then siblings, grandparents, teachers, childcare givers, and anyone else in a potentially close emotional relationship with them.

Divorce has the tendency to bring out the worst in the two individuals going through it. When angst starts to rule the roost, every reactionary word and behavior directly impacts and teaches your children similar behaviors and so conditions and aligns their subconscious core values that will affect their ways of making choices in the future. Over time, they often end up shutting down because they are hurting or possibly afraid of upsetting one or both of their parents. Children of divorce often subconsciously blame themselves for the strife and fighting of their parents. Just imagine the emotional pain and resulting stress this could cause your children!

One of the greatest concerns in all of this is that parents can be oblivious to the fact that children have the subconscious inclination to think they are the reason for their parents' arguments and eventual divorce. Imagine the guilt your children could be feeling! This "guilt" leads to a sense of overwhelming insecurity, often causing kids to shut down or go into a mode of extreme reactionary behavior.

The woeful irony is that *responsibility* for this falls on the parents. In my case, this meant me. In your case, it very well could be you. So many parents of divorce blame and shame their ex/ex-to-be or make excuses for their behavior. I am mystified why so many parents are either not *aware* of this and don't get it or don't seem to care because they make it all about themselves.

Setting a great example as a parent, especially during the tough times, can go a long way in instilling positive foundational core values in your children, nurturing their self-esteem, and teaching them to develop open two-way communication.

This begins with learning to truly listen and striving to calmly, openly, and honestly communicate with your ex/ex-to-be and definitely with your kids. It takes practice to maintain self-control in those moments when you start to get upset, angry, or frustrated. Understand that the instant you lose your cool, you have lost control of yourself and of the situation.

### Behave as If They Are Watching, Because They Are

There are two basic categories of behavior: *conscious behavior* and *subconscious behavior*. Conscious behavior occurs when you are

## WHEN KIDS SHUT DOWN OR OVERREACT

completely *aware* of what you are saying and doing and when you think things through before taking action. Subconscious behavior occurs when you unknowingly react to a *subconscious fear*.

Children learn their behavior, and lifetime conditioning occurs, from the interactions and dealings they have with the individuals closest to them. Parents have the primary impact, followed by other relatives, caregivers, and teachers. As kids get older, they often emulate their peers' behavior, sometimes because of intense peer pressure.

The psychology behind this process can be in-depth and complicated. I will lay out a basic understanding as I see it. Behavior is either *conscious* or *subconscious*. For children, *subconscious behavior* is initially formed by parents' behavioral interactions with children via the examples they set. Of course, this holds true for you and for me. Our subconscious reactiveness stems from our own childhood experiences, that caused pain which formed the foundation of our fear-based *belief system*, our *BS*.

Do you get upset and yell at your kids? Do you constantly correct them? (This was one of my personal wake-up realizations!) Do you enable your children by not following through on your disciplinary "threats"?

If you were thinking yes to any of these, reflect on your own childhood interactions with your parents. Did they react in these same subconscious ways?

Our parenting traits are often eerily similar to those of our parents', yet most of the time we don't realize we're demonstrating the same type of behavior that they did.

If your parents never listened to you, it is likely you too have become a close-minded parent who does not truly listen to your children. Listening is the basis of respect and instilling a sense of self-worth in your kids.

As I mentioned earlier, when I was a child, my father constantly corrected me. He always wanted me to do things "his way." A few times he punished me for things I had not done, and that I, in fact, knew nothing about. The most extreme of these occurred when I was about ten or eleven. Dad accused me of losing some of my mom's nicest jewelry. When I told him I didn't know anything about the jewelry, he did not believe me and threatened to punish me if I didn't find it. Not knowing anything about the missing items of value, I wandered around aimlessly trying to find the pieces. Each time I returned without the jewelry, my father punished me with a belt or hairbrush on my rear end. The impact was one of emotional and psychological trauma. After all, I had been punished for telling the truth. As I grew older, Dad would occasionally share stories from his own childhood about how unreasonably reactive my grandfather had been toward him. I realized my dad had simply been carrying out the *generational cycle* of how his father had reacted and treated him throughout his childhood so long ago.

When I reflect on my own parenting, I am amazed by how often I have automatically corrected or pointed out to my daughter how I think she should do things (which translates to doing things "my way"). No wonder she sometimes shuts down instead of asking me questions!

This has become an unconscious habit on my part and as my *awareness* has grown, I've become more determined than ever to figure out different ways to communicate and interact with my daughter.

Young children are in the stage of life where the seeds of fear are planted and subsequently deeply embedded, particularly by their parents. For their first eight to ten years, children are forming their innermost subconscious *belief system*, which they use to make most of their choices. A good analogy is that as children need to learn how to walk, their psyche needs to learn how to function. This is one of the single most important responsibilities of parenting, yet one that is done subconsciously by most parents. With heightened levels of *awareness*, parents can demonstrate more positive examples to help children form an empowering foundation from which to prepare for the future.

On the other hand, when parents lack *awareness*, they tend to teach their kids to develop *belief systems* similar to their own and to make the same mistakes they have continuously made.

Committing to break the generational cycle for the sake of your children is a conscious choice any parent can make once they "see the light." One of the biggest challenges for parents is to teach and instill integrity-based core values for children, especially during the extreme duress so often created by divorce.

This intentional shift will allow you to help your kids form the foundation for developing concrete morals and ethics, nourish firmly grounded common sense for robust decision-making skills, develop the integrity necessary to distinguish between "right and wrong," and establish and nurture two-way mutual respect in your future relationships.

When you find yourself reacting to your ex (yes, you, reacting . . . not your ex reacting to you), it's the perfect time to pause and literally go look in the mirror. The biggest reason to do this is for the sake of your kids. The second reason is to reduce your own stress. The third significant reason is that as you start to shift your behavior, over time your ex may start to shift his or her own reactive behavior. Remember, what you put out energetically is typically what you get back. When you react with anger, it is almost always because a *subconscious fear* has been triggered.

When you react with anger to either your ex or your kids, your children will tend to either react or shut down. Think about this: When someone is out of control—in this instance you—what other options are there for the other person? When someone gets angry at you, what is your inclination?

For me, it was a new challenge to become more *aware* of my fears and reflect on where they came from. Now I can focus on what I really want and how I need to intentionally be to get there or create it. This is also one of the most worthwhile things I have ever done, and it is something I continue to work on to this day. We all possess fears that, when triggered, make us react and spin out of control. But their existence doesn't mean our anger is justified, and it certainly does not mean we should allow them to be normal parts of our lives. I realized that, for me, I had to do something to figure out how to be more *aware* in order to learn how to calmly deal with those impactful situations that trigger something inside.

So I developed an *awareness trigger*, which has worked extraordinarily well for me. Each time I feel a fear being triggered, evidenced by either an emotional or energetic drain when I feel unsure or an adrenaline spike when I start to get angry, I visualize a little red flag popping out of the top of my head, as I mentioned earlier. This flag signals that I need to take a few slow, deep breaths to regain and maintain my composure. While the little red flag is waving, I suddenly know that I do NOT want to feel this way, that I do NOT want to be angry or reactive. Then I can shift to focus on what I DO want, how I DO want to feel and be. This "process" has helped me consistently shift my perspective and create more positive outcomes.

If you find yourself having lost control in front of the kids, it's important to return to integrity with yourself and with those receiving the brunt of your explosive reactiveness. Apologize to your ex and, if necessary, to your kids.

A noble goal is to have the *awareness* to be reassuring to your kids in ways that nurture them to develop self-confidence, independence, and self-assurance. This could include inspiring them to do seemingly simple actions such as sleeping alone, turning on and off the bath or shower, pouring juice, tying their shoes, and so on.

Because they are so caught up in their self-centeredness, many divorced parents fail to truly and fully listen to their children and let them know their divorce is not their children's fault. By maintaining my composure and self-control via *awareness*, I have consciously shifted how I deal with and interact with my daughter in almost every circumstance. As a result, the two of us have an open, honest, trust-based foundation for a two-way loving communication. This is something I never had with my parents, which is a major reason why it is so vitally important to me.

## The Choice of *Awareness*

*Awareness* is a learned and conditioned choice, an intentional way of being. And since it is a choice, you are empowered to make it. You either have heightened *awareness*, or you do not. As a parent, I strive to have *clarity* for what I want to teach my daughter. I understand that I teach her via my words, choices, actions, inactions, reactions, and my behavior (each and every one of these has a consequence). These include teaching Alie about developing and having *awareness* of herself and of others; to help her understand where her fears come from; and to recognize when they are in control. Now she can choose to be proactive and take more positive-oriented action to take control of her life via her own choices and be more consciously responsive in a calm, respectful, and self-empowering manner.

With my father, it was either his way or the highway. To this day, my mother reacts with anger when we have different opinions on almost anything. It is not okay with her when I disagree, which makes it extremely difficult to have an open, honest, calm discussion on so many levels. By contrast, the open, two-way-communication-based relationship I have with Alie is a blessing for both of us.

Solid and grounded ethics, morals, honesty, passion, discipline, health, and love are the main key core values I hope to teach and instill in Alie via my examples. These are the seeds I dream of planting for her so she doesn't make the same mistakes I have made.

Again, it's about breaking the *generational cycle*. These are some of the greatest gifts I can give to my precious daughter.

Most of us lack a sufficient level of *awareness* to reach these goals. People are so conditioned by parents, schools, media, and overall culture to be reactive to the situations that arise in their lives. The majority of people react to any and every person and situation, often with frustration, anger, or by shutting down. This is the very essence of the *Vicious Cycle of Subconscious Fear*. Through reacting to fear, people get more of what they are afraid of. Then they blame the resulting consequences on someone or something else.

Learning to pause and take a few slow, deep, focused breaths slows the metabolism, promotes calm, and is an impactful tool for the journey to develop heightened *awareness*, where it truly all begins.

I strongly believe that setting the best example you can cultivates *awareness* for the people in all of your relationships and will lead to more positive outcomes in all areas of life, particularly in the realm of divorce for your children. This is the concept of the *Ripple Effect of Awareness*. Your behavior affects you and the people in your life, and even beyond. When you lash out with frustration or anger, it impacts others. When you nourish someone with love, compassion, or gratitude, it affects him or her.

You cannot change anyone else. You can only work on transforming yourself to become the person, leader, and insightful and inspiring parent you desire to be. Asking someone questions is a much more effective way to help them learn, compared to telling them what you think they need to change.

## Learn from Your Mistakes

We are all working toward excellence, but this can be a long and often obstacle-ridden journey. You'll make mistakes, but you can make the conscious choice to use them as opportunities to learn and grow.

For most of my life, I was afraid to express myself. I was not consciously *aware* of this until a few years ago when I began to look within myself to see how I could improve as a parent and in all areas of my life.

I was not afraid to talk about surface topics. Rather I was afraid to share my innermost feelings about the things that are really important to me. It was a fear of expressing my emotions, including being vulnerable about sharing these very fears.

Where did these fears come from?

They were instilled and formed during my childhood. I was constantly being corrected for not doing things the right way or for not having done things my father's way. This often irrational behavior on the part of my father and the resulting extreme consequences became embedded in my *subconscious fears*. When I became a father, I was very *aware* of the impact my father had on me, and over time I began to make different choices for how I interacted with my daughter.

When we react to our *subconscious fears*, we rarely demonstrate compassion, calm behavior, listening, cooperation, or compromise. Rather, we typically set examples of fear-based reactions that tend to further fuel our anger, often regarding directly correlated control issues. Subsequently, we instill these same characteristics in our children, unknowingly teaching them to do exactly the same things that we are doing with and to them.

With heightened *awareness* of this, you can start to break the *Vicious Cycle of Subconscious Fear* by making more conscious choices that change the outcome for what happens next!

There is much more to the underlying aspect of the subconscious, which ultimately leads to your often reactive behavior. Until you start to develop heightened *awareness*, your *subconscious fear*-based "dragons" will be very powerful compared to your conscious realm of *awareness*. This is precisely why it's vitally important to work on being consciously *aware* in any given moment and choose to reflect on and learn from those moments when you do experience a lapse in judgment.

## The Pain of Divorce

Think seriously about what happened to the trust between you and your spouse when you started to go through the experience of separation and/or divorce. This is likely one of the most catastrophic, unimaginable, and painful experiences for you and your family dynamic. Even in the best of cases, it isn't even close to easy. And even in the most outwardly well-adjusted and content children, inwardly they might feel like the world is ending. Start to consider how much worse it is for your kids when you are constantly fighting and reacting to your significant other.

Start by asking yourself questions like: *Do we still treat each other with dignity, integrity and respect? Or do we show distrust, deceit, disrespect, or even disgust via outbursts of anger or outright refusal to listen and communicate? Do I remain calm, or does my anger get the best of me, making me yell at my ex often for no real reason? Do I emit love or do I emit anger, maybe even spite and hate?*

Stop for a minute . . . no, really stop.

Take a few slow, deep breaths. Now reflect on all of the newly stirred up, truly nasty, deeply rooted fears you may be unknowingly embedding in your children as a result of the examples you are setting with your behavior.

It's pretty damn scary, isn't it?

I ask you, do you have the strength and courage to look within yourself? Are your children a big enough reason for you to try to create an inner shift? I absolutely hope and pray so!

Do your kids give you the motivation, the inspiration to commit to developing a newfound level of *awareness* for your words, choices, actions, inactions, reactions, and the consequences of each? How about for the way these impact your children, yourself, and the other parent? Do you believe it's important to raise your children with love, integrity, and respect? Are you wondering how to even remotely begin to do this with all of the angst amidst your situation? You should absolutely invest the time to seriously reflect on each of these challenging questions.

The goal of this chapter is to help you recognize the undeniable and important impact your behavior, whether conscious or subconscious, has on your family. Following through on changing your fear-based subconscious reactive behavior patterns begins with love and respect for yourself, for your child, and respecting the other parent, at least as a parent.

Yes, you can respect someone even when you disagree with them, or at the very least you can accept that they are different and you cannot change them. Does it make sense to you that if you indeed truly love and respect yourself and unconditionally love your kids, then there should not be any reason or need to react to the other parent in anger? Anger is really a triggered subconscious reaction to your own internal fears.

Once again, take a few slow, deep breaths. Are you ready to begin now? If yes, why? If no, why? It is a choice, and possibly one of the most important ones of your life. Your children's emotional and psychological state of mind could be at stake.

### • Reflective Questions •
*Do the work and experience the change.*
*Be sure to write down your answers.*

- How do my children learn their behavior?
- Is it possible that my words, choices, actions, and reactions may be leading to my kids shutting down because they are fearful of expressing themselves?
- If yes, why am I doing this, and how can I stop doing it?

- What is the best way for me to instill positive core values in my children? (Hint: Through your words and personal example).
- How can I become aware of and learn more about my fears?
- How can I make sure I do not pass on my fears to my children?
- What triggered my realization that I am behaving or reacting to my kids like my own parents did with me (and more so than I ever thought possible)?
- What do I really want to teach my children?
- Am I teaching this to them?
- Why is awareness so rare in our society?
- How can I ingrain heightened awareness within myself and my children?

## CHAPTER 7

## EMOTIONAL DISTRESS

Emotional distress occurs inside children of divorce as a result of the drama and trauma emanating from their parents' angst-driven behavior. As shared earlier, many children think they are to blame for their parents' divorce. This may make them shut down or do the opposite—become reactive "problem children." Underlying, dark emotional fears often lead to subconscious conditioning that can impact your children for the rest of their lives. As a parent, what could be worse than causing emotional distress in your children? It can be tough to admit when you've made mistakes that have led to this type of damage.

When it comes to raising kids, particularly in the realm of divorce, there are many ways in which parents unintentionally create pain within their children, for themselves, and to the other parent. Two key questions to ask yourself are: 1) *What kinds of emotional distress do I observe in my children?* and 2) *What are the ways I cause this distress?*

Emotional distress is a subconsciously conditioned mechanism within the psyche that causes confusion, frustration, anxiety, sadness, depression, or anger. The trigger is typically subconsciously conditioned over time from the example parents set during situations and interactions.

## SPLIT HARMONY

Causing emotional distress in your children is an unconscious consequence of your behavior via your words, choices, actions, inactions, and reactions. To create a positive shift, first be *aware* of how your anguish is coming out and potentially impacting your kids. Second, forgive yourself for those moments when you lose self-control and react, especially with anger and hurtful or spiteful intent, and then find a better way to move forward to the best of your ability. Finally, strive to learn from your mistake(s) and to be more *aware*, calm, and in control.

There are times I have not listened, been frustrated, yelled, not followed through on a promise, or said something negative about Alie's mother, which are all ways I have unknowingly planted seeds of emotional and psychological distress in Alie. For instance, Alie would get excited about something, such as a great gymnastics session. Typically, when she tried to share her excitement with me while I was in the middle of something else, I did not give my utmost attention to her. She would then leave the room very disappointed and even despondent. In response to this, my goal became to pause and give her my complete attention.

Today, when I promise Alie we will do something, I make sure we do it. In the past, I did not always have a high level of *awareness* and subsequently did not follow through on some of my promises.

I want to teach Alie by setting the example that following through is a part of integrity and therefore extremely important. This includes being on time, which is something I believe is a matter of respect to those I've made a commitment to. Being *aware* is the initial key to limiting any emotional distress I cause in and for my daughter. Stopping, thinking, and then acting is a must.

It is important to remain calm, stop, and think before blurting out your thoughts. It's also essential that your children know you love them unconditionally, want to pay attention to them, and will hear what they are saying. It is possible to heal a portion of the internal pain you've caused if you have the *awareness*, desire, and make a conscious effort to do so.

## It Starts with Listening

The easiest way to begin to reduce the emotional stress you cause your children is to listen to them. Otherwise, how would you have any idea about the impact you have on them? Listening is such an important trait and skill, yet so rare in our society. When you want your kids to listen to you (or to anyone), doesn't it make sense to set the best possible example for them?

Being a good listener takes self-*awareness* to admit that you are not a good listener in the first place. Most of us aren't all that great at it. It also takes an ongoing commitment to learn how to be a good, reflective listener. A great book about listening is *The Lost Art of Listening* by Michael P. Nichols, PhD.

In reflecting about my own listening, I realize there are several people in my life I find extremely challenging to listen to because my triggers have become way too sensitive. This is quite a revelation and a great basis on which to commit to make a concentrated effort to listen and accept, not judge. There's no better place to begin than with those you find listening to the most difficult!

When you learn to truly listen, your relationship with your kids can markedly improve, as can any relationship, including with the other parent of your children. What an incredible gift to the kids! Listening nurtures meaningful communication and leads to forming a foundation of respect for any relationship.

True listening means just that: listening completely without interrupting and acknowledging that you've heard and understood what they've said. One of the best ways to do that: after your child is done sharing, verbally summarize what you heard.

Children are often more *aware* than you give them credit for. When parents consistently do not listen to them, children may start to build and harbor deep resentment. A child's subconscious can begin to take over, and they often go to dire measures to make sure their parents pay attention to them.

Examples of this could include getting in trouble at school, suddenly receiving poor grades, inflicting self-pain, causing major scenes of misbehavior in public, threatening to leave, or even disappearing for a few days. Such behavior can go to extremes. The longer no one is listening, the greater the resentment builds inside of kids.

Eventually children can start to subconsciously shut down and not express themselves, especially to their parents. Would you continue to try to communicate with someone if they never listened to you—or worse, didn't believe you if you were telling the truth?

The most important factor is to strive to hear what your child is attempting to express. Kids love to share their joy and often hesitate to express their frustration. Be *aware* of what they are saying and how they are saying it. This can be helpful for discovering any potential underlying message or cry for help.

For you as a parent, this translates into being present for your children and making a consistent, true effort to understand, have empathy, or at times simply accept what a child is saying without being judgmental or reactive, or without sharing your opinion.

This can be challenging, but committing to this effort can be transformational for your relationship with your children. It can form a foundation of absolute and deeply rooted trust and respect with your children—a foundation built on integrity and the intentions of unconditionally loving, open, honest two-way communication.

A favorite descriptive term of mine is *purposeful misinterpretation*. When you purposefully misinterpret what someone has said, it is purely and simply to feed your own ego or support your fears. This rarely does anything positive, especially when you react with anger in an aggressive manner. When you disagree, rather than argue, simply

# EMOTIONAL DISTRESS

listen and accept that the other person has a different opinion. When you do this, you can move forward in a much more positive fashion.

## Angst-Fueled Reactions Cause Emotional Distress

Children endure a rather exorbitant amount of emotional distress from various sources as they go through childhood. A major cause directly results from how their parents interact with them and with each other. Over time, this can result in your kids having low levels of self-esteem and self-confidence and lead to having high levels of reactiveness.

The seeds of emotional distress often result from the ways you overreact to situations, especially the more challenging and difficult circumstances life brings to the table during separation and divorce.

An insightful way of looking at this is that most of us have been conditioned to react with anger, resentment, frustration, or out of spite (with revenge in mind) to life's challenges. These reactions stem from *subconscious fear*.

Your children are no different. Your precious loved ones, especially up until the age of eight to ten, are in the very midst of their subconscious conditioning, most of which comes from you and their other parent. Kids do not have any *awareness* of the fears being formed within their subconscious. When they react to scenarios, whether it is shutting down or being out of control, they are not thinking at all. Rather, their subconscious is driving their reactionary behavior.

Because of their unawareness and innocent naiveté, when faced with unpleasant circumstances, children's fears can be overwhelming for them, causing dire emotional distress.

Over time, these fears can be deeply embedded even further unless you strive to learn how to help your children become more *aware* of their *subconscious fear* and how it can adversely impact decision making throughout their lives. Helping them become more *aware* of their *subconscious fear* is especially critical as they grow older.

Unless you can more positively impact your children by setting the best possible examples for them, including having meaningful communication skills, these deeply embedded fears can affect how your children deal with situations, including marriage and their own parenting experience, in the future.

**Being Combative Causes Emotional Distress**

Many children of divorce find themselves caught *in the middle* between their parents, both of whom they cherish and love. When your children are forced into the midst of combative scenarios ignited by the differences resulting from you and your ex's contradictory opinions, it causes them great emotional distress.

The resulting emotional distress is not caused by the differing viewpoints; rather it is inflamed by one (or both) parents' insistence that they are right and the other parent is wrong. The ensuing inflammatory anger fuels argumentative interactions between the two of you. This immediately puts children *in the middle*, causing a push-pull reaction of emotional distress, confusion, and often resentment toward one or both of you.

Over time, this can build up and turn into an emotional time bomb within your children. Let me share a specific personal example. When Alie was younger, I volunteered to be the assistant coach of her soccer team. At the end of one game, the opposing coach approached me to let me know some of our players had been calling his players names. This display of poor sportsmanship did not sit well with me or with our head coach. We discussed good sportsmanship and how we should handle the circumstances with our team of eight- to nine-year-olds. The head coach composed an email and sent it to the players' parents.

We talked to the players as a team and asked them to let us know when any poor sportsmanship, such as name-calling, bad-mouthing, swearing, kicking, or yelling, was exhibited by any of our players.

## EMOTIONAL DISTRESS

Our goal as coaches and parents was to help instill solid morals and ethical behavior—the basic foundation for good sportsmanship both on and off the field—which is so rare in today's world.

This is challenging enough for parents, much less for the coaches of a soccer team of eight-year-olds. We hoped to receive the support of each and every parent. This support was indeed received via individual email responses from parents and continued with personal comments in the form of thanks and praise from parents during the next few practices and games. The parents of the child who had specifically demonstrated subpar sportsmanship personally thanked us for how we handled the situation.

But not everyone shared these sentiments. I was horrified to find out that my ex-wife had called our daughter a "snitch" for honoring our request as coaches to "tell on" her teammates who did not live up to our code of conduct. Can you even begin to imagine the confusion, inner turmoil, and emotional distress our daughter felt at being called a snitch by her own mother after having done exactly what her coaches (and her father) had asked her to do?

Why would any parent call their child names? Why would a parent not be supportive of the coaches in such a difficult situation, even if they disagreed with how things were handled? A parent resorting to name-calling exhibits poor sportsmanship in life and in parenting.

I was proud of my daughter for sharing details of the poor sportsmanship demonstrated by her teammates. She expressed that she already felt like a tattletale. We talked about the situation in-depth. Even though she did what the coaches had asked the team to do, she had found it hard to follow through on our request. She had done so because she knew we felt strongly that this was the best way to help the team foster good sportsmanship. We also talked about her mother calling her a snitch, which really made her feel terrible about herself—it also made her feel that her mother was deeply disappointed in her. This is a hard pill to swallow for any child.

Alie was being commended by her coaches (and her father) on one hand, and on the other was being completely put down, embarrassed, and told she was wrong by her mother. Turmoil. Confusion. Emotional distress. Stress. Resentment. Can you think of anything else that may have been going on inside of her?

This illustrates how an utter lack of *awareness* on the part of parents can create major emotional distress in children, whereas working to have a higher level of conscious *awareness* will lead to eliminating or at least lessening potential emotional distress.

Instead of telling my daughter that her mother was wrong and putting Alie further *in the middle*, Alie and I discussed how it's okay for parents to have different opinions. I reassured her that I was very proud of her for doing what her coaches had asked and that I knew it had been hard for her to come to us in the first place.

I asked her how she felt when her mother called her a snitch. She said she felt terrible and that she didn't feel like she should share things with her mom because her mom always got upset. I let Alie know this was understandable. I said her mom probably really did not know what had happened and was simply reacting.

I don't know if I handled the situation in the best possible way. I do know I could have further raised my daughter's emotional distress if I had told her that her mother was wrong or if I said negative things about her mom (which I certainly was feeling and thinking). If I had confronted her mother about the situation and caused a scene or argument, it would have led to more emotional distress for Alie.

I was striving to be my best and to be *aware* of Alie's needs and her emotional distress and be supportive of her. I made the conscious effort to not be condescending about her mother's own reactive behavior.

When the actions of parents put children *in the middle*, kids are often unintentionally put in an emotional distress incubator. When parents are constantly reacting to their ex/ex-to-be, they are

## EMOTIONAL DISTRESS

doing many other things that can ignite, and even worse, fuel this emotional distress.

### Be the Example You Want to See in Your Children

By setting a positive example for your children, you help to instill similar aspects of integrity in them, and you'll be more likely to receive it back from them. The intentions, thought processes, and resulting energy you emanate in life, including to and for your children, are what you get back.

Be consistently *aware* that the struggles and difficulties you experience during situations of separation and divorce directly impact and affect your children, often in ways you have never considered.

Constant anger, verbal bashing, or belittling of the other parent can result in deeply embedded anger, resentment, and fear in a child's subconscious. This resentment can be for the parent demonstrating such behavior, for the other parent being blamed, or for both. This can develop into an unstable emotional powder keg waiting to explode, especially later in life.

One of the absolute worst things any parent can do is to purposefully try to alienate their children from the other parent. Points of "leverage" that are used to do this include threatening to withhold money from the kids or intentionally and directly saying untruths to the kids about your ex/ex-to-be. To me, both of these actions are heinous and absolutely inexcusable. To help minimize emotional stress for your children, several characteristics are essential.

First, be *aware* of yourself, of your child, and of the ways you have allowed the other parent to push your hot buttons. Listen—really, truly listen. Be sure you are hearing what your child or the other parent is saying, what they are really trying to express. Often issues lie underneath the words. During such times, *awareness* can transform the outcome. When you disagree with the other parent, do not outwardly disagree by making accusations or sharing your disparaging opinion.

My favorite response when I disagree with my ex is to simply say, "Thanks for sharing." This also disarms any further imploding commentary from either Kathy or me.

For children, discipline and consequences play an important role in instilling values and developing two-way, mutual respect with parents. The "how" of the consequences need to be consistent with open and honest expression beforehand regarding why you are punishing your child. Following through on previously stated consequences is so important. Idle threats lead to your future threats being absolutely meaningless and no lessons being learned. "Consequences" does not mean using physical or corporal punishment.

True, loving, open, and honest communication is simple in concept, yet more difficult to practice. Effective communication can be broken down into 10 percent what you are trying to say and 90 percent how you are saying it. An example of this would be how you react when you are really angry. You can yell, scream, throw, hit, make accusations, deny, threaten, and so on. Or you can express your anger with loving intent, by telling your children or your ex how angry you are while remaining calm and using appropriate words, all the while maintaining self-control.

## Be Supportive

What about support—support of your child and of the other parent? It seems like a basic concept, yet so many parents completely ignore it. Showing support for your ex (especially in front of your children) goes a tremendous way in reducing emotional distress and comes back in the form of support for you.

An example of this appeared earlier in this section when the poor sportsmanship incident occurred. Instead of telling your child the other parent is wrong, you can let them know that it's okay to have

## EMOTIONAL DISTRESS

different opinions and that moms or dads do not always handle situations the same way.

Let them know that you and the other parent are each doing the best you know how. If your children are old enough, you can even explain that you realize this is giving them dissimilar examples and that as they grow older, they will be able to make their own decisions regarding how to handle situations, hopefully by remaining calm and maintaining self-control.

Instead of reacting with anger in the moment, a more effective mode of communication would be to calmly yet firmly let your ex-spouse know you are really upset and you disagree with her or him. Further, let them know you feel it would be best to continue the discussion at a later time when you have both calmed down.

Wouldn't this be a better example to set for your children? Self-control is a wonderful gift to demonstrate to your kids via your example.

Through being *aware* of these potential skills and consistently utilizing them, it is possible to reduce and keep emotional distress to a minimum for your children. The glorious irony is that you will cause less stress for yourself and even for the other parent, often by simply giving them less reactive stimuli.

If your initial thought here was that you do NOT want to reduce stress for the other parent, stop and think about this for a minute. By reducing stress for your ex, you are reducing stress for yourself. The more stress you cause them, the more reactive they will be and vice versa. Over time, as you shift your behavior to cause less stress, the less reactionary they will be.

### Keep the Lines of Communication Open

The ability to avoid underlying turmoil arising from substantial emotional distress often boils down to having open and honest communication. Imagine the potential damage to your child's psyche when you tell them they are not allowed to talk about something that is really bothering them.

The resulting fears and hesitation a child could feel in such a situation can become acutely ingrained. If your children cannot figure out what they are "allowed" to talk about with you, they may end up completely shutting down out of fear.

One of my absolute main priorities as a parent is to always have an open, nurturing communication-based relationship with my daughter. Just because I might want to avoid, or am tired of, a topic, especially one that is truly troublesome to her, I still want her to know it is okay to talk with me about it.

I want to help Alie grow and learn to be expressive in open and honest ways. I want to cultivate her self-confidence and her desire to be expressive. This will help minimize any potential inner turmoil that could stifle her ability to communicate in the future.

Alie and I have an agreement that no matter what she asks me, I will always tell her the truth. I can relate to the fear some children have of expressing themselves because I lived it as a child. I was not allowed to talk about things my father did not want to hear about or discuss. It was always my father's way or no way.

I want to reassure my daughter, not make her afraid to talk to me. To reassure her and build her self-confidence, I need to listen to her and hear what she is saying. At the end of the day, this recipe to reduce emotional distress is not a difficult one to follow. It is prescriptive: It calls for balance and careful thought and putting the needs of your children well above your own personal needs and emotions. It isn't always easy. Sometimes it is downright hard. It calls for you to apologize, remain patient, pragmatic, respectful, and do all you can to consider how you react, especially when the going gets tough.

You can do this. Listen, love, and remember that you and your ex/ex-to-be are the most significant influences in your children's lives. You have an endless and remarkable impact on the development and growth of your children. Good or bad, your children will adopt your habits and behaviors. So make sure your examples count.

## • Reflective Questions •

*Yes, it's true! By doing the work, you will grow and change. With that said, commit to doing the work ... write it down!*

- If the other parent does or says something that causes emotional distress for your children, when it is brought to your attention, how can you help the kids deal with feelings of inadequacy, disappointing others, or worthlessness?
- When you realize you have caused emotional distress for your children, is it too late or is there anything you can subsequently do to help alleviate the inner turmoil that may be going on inside them?
- How effective are your listening skills regarding your children? How are these skills with others?
- Why would you want to be an effective listener?
- What and how can you shift to become an effective, compassionate listener?

# CHAPTER 8

## EMOTIONAL ABANDONMENT

The natural progression of emotional distress leads to emotional abandonment. Emotional abandonment occurs when a parent intentionally or unintentionally cuts off emotional support to their children. Various scenarios for how this might occur include a parent literally abandoning his or her family without any further communication.

Several examples include self-centered parents who do not spend quality time with their children, do not let their children express themselves, or do not believe their children when they are telling the truth. As children grow older, many parents try to control them or do not make any attempts to nurture true two-way open communication. When a child is emotionally abandoned, he or she might end up with a deeply embedded empty feeling and a void of love and might potentially harbor deep psychological resentment and anger throughout their lives. This can lead to major challenges or even disaster later in life, particularly in the teenage years.

Looking back over the time since our divorce and reflecting on whether I have ever emotionally abandoned my daughter, I would have to say I did so more than a few times. When my daughter is with me (which is half the time), I want to be emotionally available to her and for her. Though I attempt to make sure I have the *awareness* to listen to her, at times I've missed some cues and not done a very good job of being there for her.

During a child-visitation-schedule dilemma with my ex-wife, I would occasionally grumble about how terrible I thought the schedule was. A few times, I intimated that I did not comprehend how Kathy could not see how bad this every-other-day parental visiting schedule was for our daughter.

By saying such things, I was inadvertently putting Alie directly *in the middle*, making her feel uncomfortable about expressing herself to me and fearful that I would say something negative about her mom. This was a truly powerful epiphany for me.

As a result, Alie has tended to keep her feelings and emotions bottled up inside, causing confusion and frustration to build. To make matters worse, in the parental visit controversy, her mother would not allow her to mention the schedule topic. Not being allowed to talk about it, Alie had nowhere to release her anxieties. I can only imagine the frustration that must have been building up inside of her.

I have wondered how this combination must have been forming Alie's underlying subconscious *belief system*. I shudder to think about the role I played in this. Fortunately for Alie, she could talk about her fears, confusion, and frustration with an individual she felt comfortable around. Having someone in her life to truly listen to her was and is a godsend for her and is something profoundly helpful for all children.

Once I realized I had sometimes emotionally abandoned my daughter, it became extremely important to me to work on being present and more *aware* of what I say and how it affects Alie. I now know that at times it is absolutely more important for me to listen than to share my opinion, especially when sharing my impressions puts Alie *in the middle*. I want to set the example for her that it's okay to talk with me about anything, not condition her to keep her emotions bottled up. I want to nurture her inner personal and emotional growth, not stifle it.

## It Might Not Be Easy, But It Is Important

Not taking things personally means that no matter what someone says or does, you recognize that their words, opinion, or reaction have nothing to do with you. Many people find this concept difficult to grasp. They believe whatever was said has everything to do with them, and they allow it to trigger their own internal *belief system*. When you understand this, it becomes easier to focus on maintaining self-control and remaining calm during duress-filled situations. This allows you to be more capable of stopping, thinking, and acting instead of reacting to your *subconscious fear* with anger, being defensive, frustrated, and so on.

By putting this into practice, especially when your ex may intentionally be trying to get under your skin or be hurtful, you can change the outcome of what will happen next. This is much more beneficial for you as you can now deal with the given situation in a less reactive and more optimistic manner, which tends to diffuse the angst for both of you.

First, you will have saved yourself a ton of stress, which has a powerful, positive impact on your health.

Second, you will not give the other person the satisfaction of your getting angry and losing control.

Third, you will be setting the best possible example for your children, whether they are present or not.

And finally, you will make your children feel as if they are emotionally supported instead of abandoned.

It's easy to understand this concept in theory. The challenge is making it a reality during the interactions with your ex as your buttons are more easily pushed in situations when you disagree.

*Awareness* is the key to remaining calm and being your best for the worthwhile challenge to not take things personally.

I strive to keep my daughter from going through such additional stress, whether it comes from me or from her mom. The side benefit: I have set a much better example. Setting the example yourself is one of the best ways to teach your children to not take things personally. As they grow older, you can start to talk about the concept and the impact it will have on them and those around them. The challenge is to incorporate this impactful concept into your daily life, making it part of your *awareness* and subsequently more conscious behavior. You must start with practice if you are ever going to be consistent!

When you fail to recognize the shift you can create in your life and in your children's lives and continue to take the things your ex says and does personally, you will most likely remain in a subconsciously angst-based reactive state. When your children experience you relentlessly reacting with anger and frustration to their other parent, they may end up being afraid to express themselves to you. This is another form of emotional abandonment.

## Self-*Awareness* Is Where It All Begins

When a parent, intentionally or unintentionally, leaves the family nest, severe trauma can result for the children and the entire family. How the remaining parent handles the situation will either help alleviate or worsen the emotional agony for their kids. Being *aware* of your subconscious state, especially if it is being triggered by anger, resentment, and frustration, is more important than ever. When the committed parent feels abandoned, they tend to blame the parent who left and then try to alienate the kids against the parent who "flew the coop."

Self-*awareness* is essential to understanding the potential impact of underlying anger-fueled words, choices, and actions on your kids. Again, I call this the *Ripple Effect of Awareness*. Taking personal *responsibility* for your behavior will create a much more positive environment for your children while simultaneously teaching them about *responsibility*. Blaming the other parent will spawn a similar, more reactive, and unstable emotional state of being for your offspring.

If the other parent's reason for leaving pertains to you, whatever the case, do your absolute best to let your children know in the most loving way possible that the other parent's leaving had nothing to do with them. Let them know it had everything to do with the parent and their own insecurities in life, that the two of you had challenges getting along, or whatever the basis.

The age of children can absolutely make a difference for how much of the actual truth, if known, is disclosed. *Awareness* is vital to making a good decision as far as what to say (disclosure) and whether it is in the best interests of the children. True two-way, interactive listening is one of the best ways to really get to know your children. Communication with loving intent has become all too rare in today's world, so be sure to do your part within your own family.

Emotional abandonment opens up an entirely new aspect for why it's important to strive to learn to be *aware* to not take things personally, especially when it comes to your children's other parent. When you start to grasp the concept of not taking things personally and apply it to your daily life, not only will it help your children, it will help you tremendously in every aspect of your life. Stress and anxiety will lessen, fewer arguments will ensue, happiness can blossom and begin to fill your days, and your personal productivity could very well begin to soar. Someone else's angst has nothing to do with you. It has everything to do with them and their life's experiences and conditioning.

When you do not take things personally and continuously focus on being present and *aware* when engaging and connecting with your child, it's easier to take more conscious actions in each situation, thus changing the outcome for yourself, for others, and particularly for your children. This will help ensure that your child remains in a positive state and doesn't develop emotional abandonment issues.

### • Reflective Questions •

*Write down your responses and thoughts for the greatest insight. Do the work, experience the growth, and create* split harmony.

- What does emotional abandonment mean to you?
- Have you ever emotionally abandoned your children? How?
- What can you do to help your children heal emotionally?
- What does it mean to not take things personally?
- Do you think the concept is realistic? Do you believe some people have intentionally tried to hurt you?
- What can you do when people react with the intent to hurt you?
- How can you teach your children to not take things personally?
- How do you think your life would change if you stopped taking things personally?

# CHAPTER 9

# THE PITFALLS OF PARENTAL COMPETITION

In endless ways, parents of divorce become competitive as regards to their children. In the previous chapters, we focused on how parents' actions and decisions can create emotional instability and distress. Much of this originates from the "competitive spirit" we often see within a divorce. It can become quite complicated, but without a doubt, there is a substantial trickle-down impact on children of divorce.

This behavior often comes in the form of telling your children, and/or the other parent, that you have done more for them, such as buying more or nicer clothes, taking them places, or letting them do something special. It also occurs when you tell a child you do not approve of something the other parent has done or said; when you focus on having custody of the children more than the other parent (or not following the agreed-to schedule); when you do not let the children call or see the other parent when you have them over; when you tell your children all the things you will do for them that the other parent won't; and when you threaten your ex if he or she doesn't do something your way.

An endless list of competitive possibilities exists. Whether advertent or inadvertent, we are all likely competitive in some way. For instance, at first I was extremely competitive with my ex-wife. Then I realized I needed to admit that I had been in denial about my competitive streak and that I had no idea of its potential ramifications on Alie.

One example that comes to mind involves the custody scheduling dilemma for when Alie was with me or her mom. When Alie told me she did not like the schedule, she also shared that her mom blamed the situation on me. I couldn't believe it. Instead of remaining calm, I immediately reacted with a completely defensive, accusatory posture. Fueled by anger, I was explosively competitive with my ex, which served to further deepen the emotional confusion for my daughter.

I told Alie I did not understand why her mom would not talk about the schedule with me, and that I had been trying for over a year to work with her. After having a conversation with a professional child psychologist, I let my ex know that the psychologist had specifically told me that an every-other-day schedule is terrible for a nine- or ten-year-old child because it provides zero stability for the child.

Parental competition stemming from anger is one of the worst scenarios, especially for your children. If I had consciously chosen to maintain a heightened state of *awareness* instead of operating in a fear-based, self-centered, reactive, competitive mode, I would have been able to maintain self-control and respond in a much more positive way. I could have said that I did not know why her mother said such things, but we were both trying our best to work things out and would continue to do so.

By consciously stifling your own typical reactive retort, you can minimize your competitive reactions to the other parent. Over time, as you shift your behavior, your ex will no longer be rewarded with being able to trigger your reactionary behavior and over time will tend to be less volatile as well. Make the commitment to be *aware* and start taking personal *responsibility* for your own defensiveness, inflammatory comments, etc. All this frustration and anger-fueled behavior does is add gasoline to the already flammable situation.

Multitudes of ways exist to handle these situations. Commit to

# THE PITFALLS OF PARENTAL COMPETITION

being calm and accepting. You do not need to always outdo your ex when it comes to your kids! Such competitive behavior on the part of either or both parents can put children *in the middle*, cause them emotional distress, and lead to emotional detachment. It further fuels your children's *subconscious fears* and can lead to additional confusion, frustration, and anger, all because of the inadvertent mind games so many parents of divorce inadvertently (or perhaps purposefully) play.

The resulting lack of trust between you and your ex often leads to insecurity. The subconscious tendency becomes trying to make yourself "look better" in the eyes of your kids. The reality of this oblivious and completely self-absorbed behavior is that you end up negatively affecting your children in all of the ways mentioned above and more. No positive outcomes result from extremely competitive behavior between divorced parents.

Once you recognize that you have been, are being, or about to be subconsciously competitive (or even worse, consciously competitive!) with your ex, flip your focus switch to be more *aware* of yourself and the *ripple effect* impact on your children.

*Awareness* inspires you to figure out the best things to do or say in order to deal more positively with any situation and at the very least minimize the detrimental effect on your children.

Depending upon the age and maturity level of your kids, when you realize you have screwed up, first apologize and explain that your behavior was inappropriate. Then reassure your children that you will try to be more aware of how you are handling situations in the future.

It requires personal integrity and courage to apologize to your children, to your ex/ex-to-be, or both. And yes, it takes *awareness* and humility to say you're sorry to your ex/ex-to-be, as it's not necessarily easy being the "bigger" person. This is a good starting point to establish more balance for your kids. One of the best things you can do is reflect, observe, and learn from your own behavior as well as that of your ex/ex-to-be so you can do a better job of being supportive of each other as parents versus being competitive. It is always important to reflect on your priorities regarding the example you want to set for your children. Subsequently, it is critical to exemplify the choices and behavior it takes to follow through and make these priority goals a reality for your kids.

You can cultivate a much more nurturing environment for your children when you and your ex/ex-to-be can talk about and agree on the mutual priorities the two of you want for your kids. However, know that you can only control yourself and be responsible for your own behavior as you focus on the follow-through. By letting go of your angst and being responsible for your words, actions, inactions, and reactions, you will have an extraordinarily positive and optimistic impact on your children. This is worth every ounce of effort it may take, for the sake of your children.

### The Competitive Ex: Don't Fall into the Trap

Needless to say, don't try to be competitive in return with your ex. When your ex continues to be competitive, whether directly with you or via your children, be as supportive of your kids as you can and make sure you are not reactively competitive in return. This can be challenging and difficult to anticipate. Know that you can follow through on this challenge by being as *aware* as possible. No more reacting to your ex's competitiveness! If you do slip up, admit it to yourself, forgive yourself, and move forward with heightened consciousness.

*Responsibility* begins by looking in the mirror. You must be a person of integrity to demonstrate it to others. If you are out of integrity with yourself, you are out of integrity with everyone else. Competition between parents of divorce is fairly common. Unfortunately, competition to see who can do the most for their kids, who is nicer, who is meaner, who can give their children the most, who is "in control" of the kids, and so on and so forth, is *not* healthy

## THE PITFALLS OF PARENTAL COMPETITION

for anyone, especially for your children. Sometimes this competition can turn into a material gift-giving competition. Do not go there. Why? Because you will be in a completely self-centered mode and void of integrity if you do.

When I was young, my parents seemed to think (probably subconsciously) that the best way to show love was to give us material things. I now realize that this is far from real, unconditional love, and in fact is detrimental for the lessons it instills. Though my parents did love me very much, they were unknowingly enabling me in a huge way. Through intense inner reflection, I now realize that this sort of enabling conditions a lack of work ethic, laziness, and a sense of privilege. I have worked diligently to overcome the values this behavior instilled in me. So I urge you not to ply your children with gifts to one-up their other parent. You put your children directly *in the middle* between you and your ex when you drag them into the competitive arena.

The most important thing to offer your children is a positive example through having in-depth *awareness* of the potentially disparaging aspects of parenting during the duress of separation and divorce. The starting point is to strive to be and do your best, particularly as a caring, loving, and supportive parent, not only for the benefit of your children, but for yourself and everyone involved.

If the other parent is being consciously or subconsciously competitive, you can intentionally decide not to engage in the competition. This can be challenging, especially if you have a competitive nature like I do. However, the positive effects far outweigh the effort.

Taking a few slow, full, deep breaths—breathing in through your nose and out through your mouth—can have an immediately calming effect and simultaneously help raise your level of mindfulness. Always remember to breathe intentionally. This is helpful for any situation and can be one of the simplest, most helpful, and calming things you can do during your extremely trying, frustrating, or angry moments. Why? You are taking in more oxygen, which is calming.

Divorced couples have different ways of dealing with custody, which is certainly something that leads to heated arguments and dissension. Whatever the details of your situation, being competitive over custody—that is, keeping track of who has the child for how many days—is definitely not a healthy approach for anyone, especially your children.

Parental competition negatively impacts your children in all kinds of ways. It puts them *in the middle* between the two of you. When parents are being subconsciously competitive, they are rarely considering what is in the best interests of the children. In other words, what is best for your children does not happen because the "competition" tends to create the opposite.

Why would any parent(s) consciously choose to be competitive, always trying to one-up the other parent, being self-centered instead of putting their children first?

Putting your children first requires taking off the boxing gloves, striving for true and honest communication and, when necessary, compromising. This can only start when you have *awareness* of yourself, your child, and the other parent. You can then nurture your ability to make conscious, more positively impactful decisions regarding your children. As a parent, what could be more important than having *awareness* about how your behavior affects your children, in the present and for the future, no matter what has gone on between the two of you?

### • Reflective Questions •

*Write down your responses and thoughts for the greatest insight. Do the work, experience the growth, and create* split harmony.

- What are ways you've observed other parents being competitive with each other regarding their children?

## THE PITFALLS OF PARENTAL COMPETITION

- Are you competitive in any of these ways? Other ways?
- How does this type of competitive behavior affect your children?
- How does your competitive behavior cause you stress?
- How does the competitive behavior of your ex cause you stress?
- When you realize you are being competitive, what can you do to start being more harmonious?
- When your ex is being competitive, what can you do to be less reactive and more harmonious to reduce the stressful impact on your children?

# CHAPTER 10

# THE EXAMPLE YOU SET AS A PARENT

In the past few chapters, we have discussed the importance of setting a positive example for your children. Just by reading this book, you are taking the crucial first steps to becoming one of the *aware* individuals who are committed to learning how to be the best possible parent for your children during the process, the experience, and the typical heightened stress of divorce.

If your behavior toward your ex/ex-to-be is reactively fueled by frustration and anger, worthwhile work awaits to be done. I challenge you to stop and think about what you are teaching your children. This can be a tough pill to swallow. It's hard to be your best when you're subconsciously allowing anger to lead the way. It's almost impossible to be calm and *aware* when you're angry. Remember, that which you focus on is what you get more of in return . . . including what you're teaching your kids.

Gain *clarity* for what you want for your children, then ask yourself if your conduct is creating this or something undesirable. When angst rules the roost of divorce, children are being negatively conditioned from the reactive behavior of their parents.

Couples that were once in love so often end up being unreasonably reactive during their separation. Why? Anger is typically the reason.

Putting differences aside leads to a much calmer scenario instead of the all-too-typical high-strung stress levels that tend to go with divorce.

My daughter recently shared a dramatic example of this with me. One of her high school classmates was in a debutante ball. Her father was a member of the organization behind the event. He did not let his daughter's mother (his ex) attend the event.

I was astonished and shocked. Had this father stopped to think about how this would affect his daughter? He obviously did not care about the impact on his ex. I would think his daughter would be furious with him and feel sorry for her mother.

I attended the event as my own daughter was a debutante as well. Yes, my ex was there. I would not have had it any other way. My daughter loves her mother unconditionally. This was one of the biggest evenings of her life.

How could a father who supposedly loves his daughter allow his anger toward his ex get to the point where he refuses to invite his ex-wife to be at such a special event? Anger can be so self-serving and often blinds parents of divorce to what their behavior is really doing.

A "bigger" person would certainly have invited his ex to the debutante ball. Obviously, he did not care how his decision affected his daughter and his ex. That happens when we let anger control our decisions.

## What You Focus on You Get More of . . . So Focus on Creating What You Want

Children unconditionally love their parents, though exceptions to this come in different forms. Sometimes one parent will purposefully try to undermine their children's relationship with the other parent. The anger is so heated that it blinds them to the negative ways it will affect their kids. My ultimate question for such scenarios is: Why would you ever want to destroy the relationship your children have with their other parent?

## THE EXAMPLE YOU SET AS A PARENT

One of my dearest friends shared an unbelievably heinous example of this with me. She and her ex had been divorced for a while and he really wanted to get back together with her. She kept saying no as she felt her trust had been betrayed and there was no going back.

Over time, her ex started using money to alienate their sons from her. Basically, he threatened to cut their sons off financially if they continued to be in touch with their mother. Who knows what else he was saying to them behind the scenes. When a parent says extremely negative things to their children about their mom or dad, it can emotionally and psychologically scar them.

The extreme anger-driven behavior by my friend's ex was apparently triggered by the fact that he realized he would never be able to get his wife back. Obviously, he never stopped to think about his role of *responsibility* that led to the divorce. Instead, he blamed my friend and focused his anger on her with the purposeful intent to hurt her without any regard or thought as to how his behavior and the outcome would hurt the children, now two grown young men.

When a parent really wants to be there for his or her kids, why in the world would the other parent, regardless of the situation with their ex, intentionally try to deprive the children from having a loving relationship with their mom or dad?

Though my friend has shared her struggles and emotional pain with me, it is hard to fathom the depths of her internal trauma. A mother's bond with her children is different than that of a father's. Think about the nine-month-process of pregnancy and the physical, mental, and emotional aspects of giving birth. This creates a different type of parental connection for a mother than for a father.

My friend is one of the most *aware*, caring, loving people I have ever known. She cares at such a level that she is willing to share her story, what she's gone through, the work she's done to deal with the emotional trauma and anguish to figure out how to reduce her stress, manage the grief from her loss, and find balance. Her experience and insights are invaluable to help other parents of divorce realize the impact of their anger, resentment, and retaliatory-based reactions on their children.

You cannot be self-centered if you want to be the best, most *aware*, and *responsible* parent you can be. Being the best parent (especially an integrity-based parent) is about being open, honest, and loving. It is about setting the right type of example for your children. Each and every time, anger will prevent you from being the best parent you can be. Anger results in subconscious, reactive behavior that has parallel negative consequences.

As mentioned throughout this book, what you focus on is what you get more of in return. When you are focused on your anger, you will get anger and all the side effects it causes. You will end up harming your children because you are teaching and conditioning them to be filled with anger in subconscious ways they may never be able to recover from.

Let's get back to the most foundational basics. Ask yourself, *What do I really want for my children? Is my behavior creating this for my children?* Be honest with your answers.

It is vital to be calm, rational, and honest while contemplating these two pointed questions. If you are still angry at your ex, your anger will make it next to impossible to see through the dark emotional clouds and be calm, rational, and honest with yourself.

If you (or your ex) have allowed your anger to boil over to the point where you are constantly reactive by being accusatory, vindictive, and angry and by yelling and saying extremely negative things about your ex to your children, then you have not put your children first. You are either unaware, or you don't care, that you are teaching them the very same thought processes and behavior. Period.

This may seem harsh, but being honest with yourself is important in every area of your life, especially as a parent. It's no wonder there seems to be such a lack of integrity and core values in society today!

# THE EXAMPLE YOU SET AS A PARENT

**Act as If Your Children Are Watching—Because They Are**
How many people do you know who are divorced or going through a divorce? It's hard to nail down a precise rate of divorce today. The sources I checked reported the rate to be about 50 percent over the past thirty or so years. The uncertainty seems to be whether this rate has increased or decreased.

My main question is how has divorce affected the millions of children of divorce? What have they been taught? How have they been conditioned? The answer is that your children will often mirror your behavior. Good, bad, or indifferent, they will see how you act and subconsciously follow suit. For you personally, I believe the single most important question you can ask yourself as a parent of divorce is this: *What do I want to teach my children from my behavior and how I handle my divorce situation?*

• **Reflective Questions** •
*Write down your responses and thoughts for the greatest insight.
Do the work, experience the growth, and create* split harmony.

- What do you want for your children?
- What kind of example do you think you are setting for your kids from behavior throughout your divorce scenario?
- How reactive are you to your ex/ex-to-be?
- Why are you so reactive?
- Are you blaming your ex for most of the challenges you are going through in your divorce situation?
- How often do you take personal *responsibility* for your reactive behavior?
- What is one thing you can do to shift your reactive behavior and remain calm and in control of yourself and the situation?

# CHAPTER 11

## CONSCIOUSLY CHOOSE THE SEEDS YOU PLANT

Knowing your behavior greatly impacts your children, the old adage that the apple doesn't fall far from the tree couldn't be more accurate. If your children see that you use anger to respond to challenges, then you can almost bet they will do the same.

Without giving it a thought, many parents of divorce get caught up in the *Vicious Cycle of Subconscious Fear*. They blame their partner for all their problems, separately and together, in their divorce or pending divorce. Recognizing your fears stem from childhood conditioning and have been reinforced throughout your life from previous relationships and situations is the first step to letting go of the underlying angst that has been fueling your reactive behavior.

It hasn't been easy, but I've done the work to understand my darkest fears. Now I can see how I have unknowingly allowed this fear to negatively impact my relationship with my ex-wife. By striving to have heightened *awareness*, I have become cognizant of what I really want for my daughter and subsequently can make conscious choices about my behavior to more clearly create a nurturing environment for her. This has been an empowering step in my journey.

# SPLIT HARMONY

It took a fair amount of in-depth work for me to figure out what this stifling fear was all about, where it came from, and how I'd been allowing it to control my choices and how it had been subsequently having an extremely negative impact on my daughter. What an eye-, heart-, and soul-opening revelation this has been!

I finally understand that at a young age I shut down and over time lost touch with my own thoughts and feelings because I'd been punished for telling the truth, my truth. Subconsciously, I didn't think my thoughts and feelings were worthwhile, particularly not to my father. Ultimately, my deepest, darkest fear formed . . . I did not think I was worthy of being loved.

Wow, no wonder my *dragon of fear* roared when someone was upset with me or tried to give me constructive criticism! I would shut down, turn off, deflect, be defensive, have a nasty tone, or be reactive. Eventually, in each and every one of my relationships, these *subconscious fear*-based reactions led to a backlash from the other "side," proving my fears were real. My fearful frame of mind generated reactions creating repercussions leading to a breakup, or in the case of my marriage, to divorce.

Until the past few years, I blamed each of the former special people in my life for the challenges and problems we experienced. I blamed my ex-wife for the eventual demise of our marriage. The biggest problematic oversight of this blame is that I had not ever taken any personal *responsibility* for my own *subconscious fear*-based choices and reactions.

How could this happen? Because prior to committing to do the self-work, I had not had any self-*awareness* whatsoever. I had experienced my parents blaming me—and I observed them blaming each other. The same holds true for former girlfriends and my ex-wife. They blamed me, and I blamed them. She blamed me, and I blamed her.

*Responsibility?* None of the "players" seemed to have any clue about

## CONSCIOUSLY CHOOSE THE SEEDS YOU PLANT

what this life- and relationship-changing principle of *responsibility* was, much less what it meant and how it could impact and change their relationships.

Let me ask you another question: *Why would you want to cause your children, yourself, and your ex stress?*

Stress has been described as one of, if not the greatest, causes of illness, disease, and sleep and health issues. To me, the unbelievable irony regarding stress is that it is typically self-induced. How is this possible? Because people are oblivious to the fact that they are reacting to their fears. In relationships, fear of loss tends to ignite the fuse of anger. As shared earlier, the greatest fears of loss stemming from divorce are the loss of financial security and the loss of the custody of the children.

Let me clarify something. If you're intentionally causing your ex/ex-to-be stress, you are also causing your children and yourself stress. This brings us directly back to the *Vicious Cycle of Subconscious Fear*. When you are reacting to your fears, you are putting out resistance to what you really want. Creating resistance to what you want, if indeed you know what you really want, leads to the creation of stress.

When you gain true *clarity* for what you want for yourself and *clarity* for what you want for your children, you can begin to shift your focus and your intentional actions and behavior to turn your *clarity* into reality. Yes, this begins with *awareness* and requires personal *responsibility*.

Realizing and implementing this, now you can start to consciously choose the type of seeds you want to plant in your children. You can plant the seeds of consciousness through your words, choices, actions, inactions, reactions, and behavior. And when you do, the people you love will ultimately benefit the most. These are the seeds that will reap crops sprouting from your newfound *clarity, awareness,* and *responsibility* for your words, choices, actions, inactions, reactions, behavior, and the impactful consequences of each. In his tremendously insightful book, *The Four Agreements: A Practical Guide to Personal Freedom*, Don Miguel Ruiz outlines four very important concepts we can all implement into our lives. View each one of these as a separate but powerful seed that you can plant in your consciousness to benefit yourself and ultimately your children. They are:

1. Be impeccable with your word.
2. Don't take anything personally.
3. Don't make assumptions.
4. Always do your best.

As a parent, looking at these in reverse order makes complete sense. For example, *always do your best* means that you have *clarity* for what you want for your kids and can then strive to be and do your best to create this for them.

*Don't make assumptions* focuses on not getting caught up in the *Vicious Cycle of Subconscious Fear*, since your fears lead you to make assumptions rarely based on facts. Understanding that reacting to your fears puts out resistance to what you want, it makes sense to *be your best*, not your fear-based worst.

*Don't take anything personally.* When you are striving to *always be and do your best*, you will not react to something someone else has said or done. When you assume your ex/ex-to-be is intentionally saying or doing something to piss you off or hurt you, you are definitely taking things personally and will react according to your fears. When you can shift to understand that they are reacting to their own *subconscious fears* and not so much to you, you can take a big breath and choose to remain calm.

Going back to Chapter 5 and the *Vicious Cycle of Subconscious Fear*, remember that as you shift your reactive behavior to an intentional responsive behavior, the other person, over time, will shift their

# CONSCIOUSLY CHOOSE THE SEEDS YOU PLANT

behavior because they are no longer getting the reactions from you they have come to expect. Not taking anything personally and the *Vicious Cycle of Subconscious Fear* are deeply intertwined. Stop taking what your ex is saying and doing personally and break the vicious cycle to change the outcomes.

And finally, *be impeccable with your word*. You are always setting an example for your children with your words, which are at the very core of your behavior. When you are striving to be your best, you will *be impeccable with your word*. When you step out of your *subconscious fears* and into *awareness*, you are more likely to stop *making assumptions* about what your ex/ex-to-be is saying and doing. You will be able to *stop taking things personally* and be more masterful in *being impeccable with your word*.

The *four agreements* are closely interwoven. Each of them, separately and together, can be faithfully applied and followed by having *clarity* for what you want for your children, developing enhanced *awareness*, and taking personal *responsibility* for your words and behavior and for the resulting consequences that impact you and the people in your life.

The seeds you plant in your children will prepare them for their future in either potentially disastrous or self-empowering ways. When you are *aware*, you can make the choice for which type of seeds you want to plant within the psyche of your kids. The type of seeds you choose to plant will either make the world a better or worse place. I strongly believe there is already too much hatred, spite, and lack of integrity in the world. Individually and together, let's commit to making the world a better place by being more conscious about our choices, especially when it comes to the seeds we cultivate via the examples we set for our children.

### • Reflective Questions •

*Write down your responses and thoughts for the greatest insight.*
*Do the work, experience the growth, and create* split harmony.

- Be honest with yourself and reflect on what you want for your children. Are your words and behavior creating this for them? How? How not?
- What are your kids learning about dealing with relationships as they observe the way you are handling your divorce situation? What do you want them to learn from you?
- How can the way you are dealing with your divorce make the world a better place?

# SECTION III

## NURTURING *SPLIT HARMONY*

*Split harmony* may sound like an impossible dichotomy. The bottom line is that it is absolutely possible to create a divorce environment of *split harmony*. I would hope that the source of inspiration for you would be to strive to create and nurture *split harmony* for the sake of your children. Stop the angst-sparked chaos and strive to live with compassion . . . for the benefit of your children.

# CHAPTER 12

## STEP 1: *FORGIVENESS*

*Forgiveness* is the first step to nurturing *split harmony*. This begins with *forgiving* yourself for the anger and frustration you feel for playing a role in creating the situation you find yourself in and for your reactionary behavior. A more challenging aspect of *forgiveness* involves forgiving your ex, usually because anger gets in your way. It is next to impossible to *forgive* when you are angry.

Let me explain. You do not have to accept what your ex has said or done. However, you cannot change what has happened. You can intentionally shift from a victim perspective to constructing a self-empowering viewpoint that will spawn a more positive outcome for you and your kids. As you intently focus on what you really want, you can shift out of the pit of frustration and anger. This will give you the opportunity to establish a foundation on which to build and foster a more positive environment for your family. You don't want more anguish, seemingly impossible scenarios, or more frustration. This in itself makes it worth the effort to shift your perspective and demeanor.

When you can work on having at least an inkling of desire to forgive your ex, you will begin to set yourself free from the underlying chains of deeply embedded stress that have been so inflamed by your anger, frustration, and regret.

Have you ever stopped to wonder what will happen if you do not stop harboring resentment toward your ex/ex-to-be? What will be the impact on your kids? What will be the repercussions for you? The last few chapters provide insight to help you consider these unintended but obvious results.

Resentment leads to reactive behavior that, over time, is detrimental to your and your children's health and overall well-being. Resentment rises out of the ashes of anger.

If you believe the situation between you and the person you married, that once special man or woman you were so in love with, is beyond repair and irreversible, you basically have two choices.

For whatever reason, maybe you'll choose the all-too-typical route most parents of divorce subconsciously take: letting your anger simmer until it leads to extreme reactionary behavior. This in turn triggers the fear-based rage and resentment of your former lover—the other parent of your children—and leads to a back-and-forth anger-fueled inferno that negatively impacts everyone in the family, especially your kids.

Or you can choose to put down the always-at-the-ready red-hot boxing gloves to accept what has already happened. You cannot change the past, so this really makes sense.

If you take the second, more preferential route, you can be working toward *forgiveness*. Once you make this decision, you can focus on gaining *clarity* for what you really want for your children and for yourself. In choosing this more peaceful route, you will reduce your and your kids' stress levels and experience self-growth (instead of anger stifling potential growth) to empower you to move into the future. One of the most important direct side effects is that you will be planting self-empowering seeds for your children via your self-controlled, well-thought-out example for how to deal with struggles and challenges, especially in the realm of relationships.

If you find that you and your ex are not aligned on the subject

## STEP 1: *FORGIVENESS*

of letting go of the angst between you, understand that choosing to commit to having heightened *awareness* will shift things for your children and reduce your own stress. Your ex will no longer be able to "push your buttons," and it is likely that, over time, she or he will typically shift their own behavior.

When individuals are obstinately self-centered, they are completely oblivious to what their choices and resulting behavior are doing to their children, much less to themselves. These particular parents of divorce may never let go of their fear-driven anger because it has been so engrained in them, likely since their childhood. These unfortunate individuals are potentially damaging their children in permanent ways and creating irreparable stress for themselves that can lead to serious health issues.

I remember the day I decided to no longer blame my ex-wife-to-be and started taking personal *responsibility* for how I handled the interactions between us. Unknowingly, I was moving toward the path of *forgiveness*. In other words, I chose to no longer let my ex "push my buttons." I even forgave her for the times that she had. I remember sitting at my former kitchen table when she said something to me to get a reaction. As I calmly sat there, with my head slightly tilted to the side, she curtly said, "What are you being so smug about?" I replied, "I am not being smug. I've decided I am no longer reacting to you because Alie is too important."

Over the next six months or so, the dynamics of what had been an inflammatory relationship began to shift. To this day, we are typically able to have calm discussions, especially when something concerns our daughter.

### *Forgiveness* Opens the Door to *Split Harmony*

My ability to shift away from my reactionary behavior began by taking a huge breath and forgiving myself for having allowed my fears to ignite my terse reactions. This has been a gift to Alie, to me, and to my ex-wife. And, yes, this is more than okay. It has dramatically reduced the stress I had been creating for Alie and for myself.

One of the most life-changing books I've ever read is *Radical Forgiveness* by Colin Tipping. In his book, Tipping talks about the extreme distinction between human forgiveness and Radical Forgiveness. When we feel we've been wronged by someone and believe we need to forgive that person, it is because we feel like a victim. *Radical forgiveness* will help you shift your perspective and change how you think. Personally, I now realize that I needed to go through the challenges of my divorce to grow into the person I was born to be (and, if you're a person of faith like I am, to be the person God intended me to be).

I needed to experience the pain of allowing my deepest fears being triggered so I could accept them, let them go, grow out of them, and step into my faith and self-belief.

Forgiving myself gave me the opportunity to move forward with a new outlook. Forgiving my ex allowed me to let go of my anger and start to create inner peace. This inner peace emanated to my daughter and to everyone in my life. (The *Ripple Effect of Awareness* in Chapter 15 will clarify this further for you.)

If you are so angry that you presently have no desire to forgive your ex, I highly suggest you reread this chapter and reflect on what your anger and resentment are doing to you and to your children. Your anger may lead you to believe that you want to hurt your ex, which is understandable. Stop to think about what your anger-fueled reactions are really doing to your children and to yourself.

If you want your ex to treat you with respect, do you think this will ever happen if you are constantly angry, accusatory, and yelling at him or her? Remember, the second you get angry, you have lost control of yourself and the interaction. If you are consistently angry and resentful, you have lost control of the relationship and will probably not get what you want without a major fight involving lawyers, court, and paying a ton of money.

## STEP 1: *FORGIVENESS*

So, again I ask you, "What do you really want for you and for your children?" This should be an easy question to answer. My guess? You want health, happiness, and a positive relationship that influences your children in a meaningful way.

While you cannot change the past, you can shift your perspective about the past and choose to look for the lessons to be learned and the opportunity to grow. The challenges you've endured may seem unbelievably difficult, yet it is during these dark times that the opportunities to grow abound. Accept what has happened and let go of your angst, frustration, and regret by forgiving yourself and at least trying to forgive your ex. Now you can take the next steps to start focusing on what it is you really want for your children and for yourself.

### • Reflective Questions •

*Write down your responses and thoughts for the greatest insight. Do the work, experience the growth, and create* split harmony.

- Do you think you need to forgive yourself for anything pertaining to your divorce?
- If yes, what? If no, why not?
- Why do you think you cannot forgive your ex/ex-to-be?
- If you continue to foster the angst and resentment inside of you, what are you doing to yourself? What example are you setting for your children?

# CHAPTER 13

## STEP 2: *CLARITY* OF DESTINATION: WHAT DO YOU REALLY WANT TO CREATE FOR YOUR CHILDREN?

Armed with your ability to forgive yourself and those who have caused you a great deal of pain, you can decide what type of divorce environment would be best for you, your family, and of course, your children. Ever since becoming a parent, my number one priority has been my daughter. I hope this book will inspire you to have a similar approach and attitude.

My number one goal as a parent has been to be the absolute best parent possible and to set the best example for Alie to prepare her for the future. I have had *clarity* that I wanted to instill a foundation of solid moral, ethical, honest, and healthy emotional, psychological, mental, physical, and spiritual core values so she can truly be *aware*, openhearted, and handle situations with confidence and calm. This is my personal clarity of destination. This chapter shares guidance to help you to glean your own clarity of destination.

I am *aware* that achieving these goals **begins with me**. I know I am giving an incredible gift to inspire my daughter to realize her full potential when I am setting a proactive, compassionate, positive example. By blaming my ex for the challenges between us, I was simultaneously disempowering Alie through my own anger and resentment. With honest reflection, I realize that I once reacted to my fears much more than I'd like to admit! Divorce has not changed my goals and priorities as a parent. My daughter means far too much for me to allow this to happen. This has been one of my ultimate commitments. The follow-through is what absolutely helped my ex and I foster *split harmony*.

## Building a Foundation of Love (for the Sake of Your Children)

When it comes to raising your children through the murky waters of divorce, what are your thoughts about parenting during and after divorce? Since there are so many theories and opinions on raising children, how do you know where to start?

An insightful and thought-provoking question to ask yourself is this: *Should my outlook and goals of parenting change because we are getting divorced?*

An equally reflective and penetrating question is this: *Just because I am going through the challenges of separation and divorce, why would I no longer strive to be my best, most authentic self?* In asking these questions and honestly considering your response, you can hone in on what type of life and environment you want to create for your family.

Presuming your number one goal in raising children is to BE the absolute best parent you can, it's important that you define what being the best parent you can be means to you. I have often found myself wondering why so many parents allow their priorities to change simply because they are now embroiled with their spouse during the process of separation and divorce. The short answer is that they succumb to their *subconscious fears*, which have been ignited by the threat of separation and divorce.

Couples divorce for many reasons. Something happens leading to disdain, disrespect, and distrust. Or over time, as the challenges of

## STEP 2: *CLARITY* OF DESTINATION

life, marriage, and having children happen, the love you've had for each other dissipates, and you drift apart. To me, these two generalities pretty much cover the range of what lies beneath the once white veil of love, now a seemingly black veil of spite and vengeance.

Anger and fear take over the interactions in what was once a fairy tale romance of two individuals. Something happens, the change begins, and the chasm constantly widens. One parent reacts out of fear-charged anger. The other parent **reacts** back, neither ever stopping to think about or reflect on the consequences of their behavior for themselves or for their children. Anger begets anger. Neither parent realizes that when they react with anger, they have lost control of themselves and their interaction. And in the end, everyone forgets about the great toll this behavior might take on their children. But it didn't start this way . . . so how can we revert back to a more nurturing environment, especially for our children of divorce?

Reflect back to your wedding day. I imagine that, just like for my ex-wife and me, for the two of you this special day was filled with love, joy, happiness, and feelings of excited anticipation stemming from your mutual promise for a future lifetime together. Embrace this memory from a place of gratitude (versus a place of regret and resentment).

With reciprocal love, excitement, and passion, you began to expand your family. In these early days, how did you, as an individual parent, and the two of you as a parenting team, make decisions involving your children? With and from love and respect, I would think.

Now fast-forward to the present . . . think about how things have changed! When did things start to shift from mutual love for and commitment to each other to operating from a place of angst and resentment toward each other? Is there now an underlying *"I'm going to get you!"* attitude of retaliation emanating from your fears, spewing anger and spite?

Are you blaming what's happened on your ex/ex-to-be? Surely you've heard of the saying, "It takes two to tango."

I hope and pray that you can understand how important it is to have *awareness* about the difference between your original loving intentions of yesteryear and the current potentially harsh impact resulting from your reactive behavior on your children (and on each other). Remember, your reactive behavior tends to be triggered by the seemingly constant *subconscious fear*-based reactions to each other.

Using this revealing realization, you can strive to put your children as a mutual first priority and work together regarding decisions involving them. Take the focus off yourself and whatever happened and shift it to a heartfelt emphasis on your kids. This begins by simply agreeing that it's okay to disagree.

## Meet Somewhere in the Middle

For the times it may seem impossible, compromise can work miracles. Compromising does not mean you are giving in. It simply means that you realize your kids are more important than arguing. You can even come up with a system to take turns, brainstorm another approach, or agree on a nonbiased third party to help you figure out a compromise (preferably not a lawyer, as this can cause distress and consternation, especially as the charges rack up leading to further stress, distress, and disagreement over finances).

Compromising was much easier when you were happily married, right? Most parents of divorce become subconsciously focused on what they do NOT want. Imagine the emotional confusion and angst you are causing your kids.

How can the two of you maintain the priority of doing what is best for your children? By being your best. By remaining calm and *not* reacting to your fears. By operating from a place of self-love and love for your children versus from a place of resentment and anger.

As they mature, children tend to emulate what their parents

## STEP 2: *CLARITY* OF DESTINATION

have done. After all, this is the example that has been demonstrated for them over and over. So how do you shift to create a healthy environment of divorce for your children?

How do you want to go down the path of divorce in raising your children? What impact do you want to have on your children as a result of your own behavior? One of the most significant epiphanies I've ever had is that when I absolutely know what I do NOT want and focus on what I do NOT want, I get more of what I do NOT want. No wonder so many parents are miserable, unfulfilled, and unhappy. No wonder so many children of divorce face huge challenges in their own relationships later in their lives. They learned from their parents.

Start taking personal *responsibility*. Resist the temptation to blame your ex. Commit to have the *awareness* to shift from what you do NOT want to focusing on WHAT YOU DO WANT. Reflect and do the work to gain true *clarity*. Visualize it. Be the person you need to be to create what you want for your children and for you. This angst-free shift will amaze you. So, what are your goals and priorities for your kids as you move through divorce? Begin by asking yourself if they have really changed.

### • Reflective Questions •

Note: *Change begins with gleaning **clarity of destination**. As a parent, this means knowing what you want to create for your children. Yes, change takes work; it takes working on you. When you do the self-work, you will start to experience a shift. To create the greatest shift, it is vital to write your thoughts down in a journal. This turns fleeting thoughts into something material, something real that you can review from time to time to see how you are progressing.*

- What do you really want for your kids? Be sure to write this down.
- What kind of parent do you want to be for your children?

- What kind of parent do you want your ex to be for your children?
- Have your parental goals changed because of the situation between you and your ex/ex-to-be? If so, how?
- How would you describe the situation between you and your ex/ex-to-be?
- How do you think the situation between the two of you is affecting your kids?
- How much stress is this causing you? Your children?
- Are you open to having a calm discussion about the above questions with your ex/ex-to-be?
- In what ways are you being supportive for your ex to be the best parent they can be? In what ways are you creating obstacles for them? Be honest!
- With your newfound awareness, what type of "seeds" are you planting in your children's emotional and psychological subconscious via your behavior?
- What is one thing you can change about your perspective and your resulting behavior moving forward?

# CHAPTER 14

## STEP 3: *AWARENESS:* WHERE IT ALL BEGINS

With a strong plan in place, you can begin to execute your focused goal of setting a positive example for your children through thoughtful behavior and nonreactionary actions. In each moment of potential conflict, you have the opportunity to be *aware* of your feelings and then use that steady and insightful *awareness* to dictate your very next steps.

One of the most powerful realizations I've ever had is that having *awareness* of my words, choices, and actions (or reactions) is the start to changing outcomes and shifting relationships. Why? Because everything I say, do, or don't do has a consequence. You must first have heightened *awareness* in order to move past blaming someone else and to start to take personal *responsibility*. Since *awareness* is where it all begins, let's get clear on the meaning of the word. Two relevant definitions of *awareness* are:

1. Having or showing realization, perception, or knowledge
2. The fact or state of being aware or conscious, especially of matters that are particularly relevant

It is essential to be *aware* of the example you are setting for your children, especially during the process of separation and divorce. Yet most parents of divorce get so caught up in their own angst and BS (fear-driven *belief system*) that they become oblivious to what they are teaching their kids via their inflammatory reactive words and behavior. But this aha moment can inspire you to create a shift in your perspective and your behavior. Of course, this presumes that your children are your top priority as a parent of divorce.

For me, realizing I had been subconsciously prioritizing my anger over my daughter became my big enough reason, my *origin of inspiration*, to put down the all-too-conventional "boxing gloves." When I was unknowingly allowing myself to react to my fears, I was not in control of my words or behavior. This life-changing epiphany led me to better understand that I am the only individual *responsible* for my words, choices, and actions (especially during times of duress). If I need to apologize to get back to a place of integrity with myself, with my ex, or with my daughter, I do so immediately and with heartfelt sincerity.

Through having *awareness* versus being in a reactive state, I have been able to make conscious choices leading to more positive outcomes for my daughter, for me, and for everyone involved. What a gift!

Without personal mentors sharing the insights from their experience, knowledge, and expertise, it might have been an insurmountable challenge to make that shift. When it comes to finding the right mentors, start by asking respected friends and acquaintances who they recommend or by doing research on the internet. Be *aware* that friends with a negative mindset fueled by their own fears and anger will NOT be helpful and may lead you to someone who can make the situation even more inflammatory.

There are public charities that have the mission to assist children and parents of separation and divorce, such as Kids in the Middle, located in St. Louis (kidsinthemiddle.org).

## STEP 3: *AWARENESS*

Your church can be a good place, as many pastors and priests offer family counseling.

Having an *aware*, integrity-based, and constructive counselor will make a tremendous difference when you are open to it.

Understand it takes a bigger person to admit they need assistance than going it alone. This requires being vulnerable. Men tend to find this more challenging. I would say most men believe vulnerability is a weakness. Nothing could be further from the truth. The ability to be open and vulnerable is a life-changing strength. And yes, it takes *COURAGE* to be open and vulnerable, especially at first.

It may take some time and *awareness* to realize which individuals and resources will be helpful. There is a lot of *BS*, fluff, and negativity out there. Know the type of core values you are looking for in a mentor/counselor.

Recognizing the fear within you requires in-depth *awareness*. Once you can admit that fear has been causing you to react, you can ask, *Where does this fear come from and how has it conditioned me?*

This is a huge step forward and one of the single most worthwhile self-realizations you may ever have.

Some fears may be overcome, while others may seem like lifetime demons. By having the *awareness* that when you are caught up in your fears, they disempower you, you can start to shift your focus to what you want and make more conscious choices leading to more positive outcomes regarding the interactions with your ex and children.

### Developing *Awareness* Takes *COURAGE*

Developing *awareness* is no easy task. But when you care deeply for your children, you will start down this road. With heightened *awareness* for how my choices were affecting me and the people closest to me (and around me), with proverbial hindsight I began to understand that I was setting a poor example for Alie by constantly putting her *in the middle* of her mom and me.

I realized the imperative need to continue to work with someone who could provide constructive insight and guidance to support and teach me to have more truthful inner reflection and lead me to gain *clarity* regarding what I wanted for my daughter. This would give me the reason and inspiration to focus on maintaining self-control, for my sake and, more importantly, for Alie's benefit.

I scheduled an appointment with Tom C., the last counselor my ex and I had seen together. Initially, it seemed he was being helpful. After about a year and a half, I became *aware* that I was consistently doing most of the talking, and he was not "assigning" any work outside of our weekly time together. Each session was essentially the same. We reviewed what we'd talked about the week before, and then talked about it some more. Nothing was changing. These "sessions" were rather subjective, with no positive shifts occurring for me.

Without insisting that individuals work on themselves, how can the possibility exist for shifting the dynamics of a relationship? It takes self-work to create the inner growth that is a prerequisite for change.

Reflecting back to the times my ex and I had gone to counseling together, I realized that without a constructive approach, there'd be no change. We were each irrefutably stuck in our respective fear-based, reactive mindsets, doing nothing to foster a shift in our perspectives. We were obstinate and determined that our respective opinions were irrefutable. As a result, we never truly listened to what the other was trying to say.

Through this experience, I discovered the immense distinction between supportive and constructive counseling, and I realized that the two of us had not found such an individual, even after having been to five or six counselors!

I stopped seeing Tom C. and was able to find a constructive-centric counselor who challenged me and insisted that I do the self-work needed to generate a mindset shift, especially for the benefit

## STEP 3: *AWARENESS*

of our daughter. Thanks to elevated *awareness,* it hit home. To kindle self-transformation, I absolutely had to put in the time, effort, and follow-through by **committing** to and **doing** the self-work.

• **Reflective Questions** •

*Write down your responses and thoughts for the greatest insight. Do the work, experience the growth, and create* split harmony.

- How would striving to heighten your self-*awareness* make a difference for you and for your kids?
- I believe that without *awareness*, transformation will not occur. What are your thoughts about this?
- As a parent of divorce, what is an area of your current family situation that could shift by working on developing heightened *awareness*?
- What is one area in your relation with your ex/ex-to-be that you wish he or she would work on having more *awareness* about?
- What is one area that you and your ex/ex-to be could work together to develop more acute *awareness* that would benefit your children?

# CHAPTER 15

## STEP 4: THE *RIPPLE EFFECT OF AWARENESS*

It was hard to come to the realization that my words, choices, actions, inactions, and the consequences of each impacted my daughter and others. But once I did, I knew I had to change my thought patterns about how I made choices. I recognized this would change the consequences of my actions for our daughter, for me, for her mom, and beyond. This describes what I now call the *Ripple Effect of Awareness*.

It's all about realizing how your *mindset* leads to the choices you make and how it reaches way beyond just you. For me, I realized my now former mindset included how my negative, fear-fueled reactionary words and behavior had a *ripple effect*. I've come to understand how being more conscious as a result of making *clarity*-based choices positively impacts the man in the mirror, my daughter, her mother, and beyond and changes the *ripple effect* I had been emanating!

There is a distinct separation between self-*awareness* and *awareness* of others, yet they are very connected. I have come to realize how much my words, choices, actions, and the consequences of each affect me and the people around me. Once I began reflecting on how my behavior was affecting my daughter and her mom, I was able to start taking personal *responsibility* for the consequences of my words, choices, and actions and consciously shift from a subconscious driving force of anger and resentment to a much more conscious force spurred by *awareness* and *clarity*.

The *Ripple Effect of Awareness* is all about having *awareness* for how your words, choices, actions, inactions, reactions, and the consequences of each impact the people in your life, especially those closest to you—in particular your children. Yet the *ripple effect* spreads beyond your family. When you start to plant seeds of compassion instead of seeds of angst, you will change the future lives and relationships of your beloved children. You will be conditioning their subconscious with incredibly self-empowering emotional and psychological tools on which they can build and nurture two-way unconditional, loving, communication-based relationships, romantic and otherwise. You will nurture self-confidence, *clarity, awareness, responsibility*, caring, compassion, and mutual respect.

To help you truly grasp the concept, let me share the *Ripple Effect of Awareness* exercise with you ...

> Close your eyes, take a deep breath, and imagine that you are standing next to a large pond named the Pond of Awareness. It is an overcast, cloudy, gloomy day. The air is still, and the surface of the water is like a mirror. The pristine blue sky, cotton ball clouds, and brambly trees around the edge of the pond are reflected in the water. Out in the pond are a bunch of small sailboats. Each sailboat represents a person in your life. One of the boats represents you. What color is your boat?
>
> Glancing down to the ground on your left, you see a remarkably ugly, malevolent-looking rock. Your curiosity gets the best of you, and you bend down and pick up the rock. Wrapping your fingers around the small, sinister crag, you immediately start to feel a wicked energy stemming from

# STEP 4: THE *RIPPLE EFFECT OF AWARENESS*

your fears, causing anger and frustration to immediately move up your arm and into your body, consuming you. You can't stand the intense sensation, and without hesitation, you turn and throw the rock far out into the pond.

As soon as the large, gross pebble breaks the surface of the water, nasty ripples representing your anger and frustration begin spreading across the surface of the pond. These ripples rock and impact the sailboats—the people in your life—with the same acutely negatively consuming emotional sensation. They are not happy about this. They turn and shake their fists at you, shouting at you to stop, to cease and desist, to get away from them.

You watch the ripples toss the sailboat representing you. You feel stressed, emotionally and physically drained, disappointed, sad, and depressed. You abhor feeling like this.

The vile ripples continue moving out in concentric circles, hitting the banks of the pond, bouncing off, moving back toward the sailboats—the people in your life. The undulations continue to have their nefarious percussive force on the sailboats. No one, including you, is happy. Everyone is frustrated, reactive, and feeling stressed out.

Open your eyes and take a few slow, deep breaths to clear your mind. Now close your eyes again and visualize you are back at the same pond. Yet somehow it looks and feels more peaceful, calm, and beautiful. It is a pristine blue-sky day, with a few beautifully wispy clouds floating by. Staring at the water's surface, it looks like it's moving as you watch the clouds skimming by, moving past the reflection of the trees, the sun glistening brightly off the pristine surface of the Pond of Awareness.

Finding yourself smiling at the calm beauty, you feel serenely peaceful and happy. Looking out across the pond, you again see all the sailboats representing the people in your life. You see your sailboat. What color is it?

Looking down at the ground to your right, you see a glassy, smooth blue orb. It is alluringly magnificent. You can't help but bend down to pick it up. As soon as your fingers wrap around it, warm feelings of joy, fulfillment, gratitude, calm, and inner peace move up your arm, then flow throughout your entire being. You look up and gaze out at the sailboats, the people, and the pond. You glance down at the glowing crystal-blue orb in your hand and realize you want to share what you are feeling with the people in your life.

Peering out at the sailboats and smiling, you wind up and intentionally throw the enchanting orb as far out into the pond as you can. As it breaks the pond's surface, thoughtful, affectionate, passionate ripples begin to spread out across the Pond of Awareness. As they caress the sailboats, everyone is suddenly feeling happy, joyful, loved, and grateful you are sharing your warm feelings of joy, fulfillment, gratitude, calm, and inner peace with them. Smiling at you, they begin to wave, motioning you to join them. They want you to share more of yourself and be with you.

As the tiny, compassionate waves begin to caress your sailboat, looking around at all the other sailboats around you, you feel amazing. The ripples hit the banks and return back out into the Pond of Awareness and continue to impact lives.

You have given of yourself and are making a positive difference in the lives of everyone around you. Through your aware, intentionally benevolent words and actions, you are setting a thoughtfully contagious example. You are teaching others through your affirmative actions. You feel peaceful, fulfilled, accomplished, grateful, and are filled with self-love. You are happy.

# STEP 4: THE *RIPPLE EFFECT OF AWARENESS*

Inhale deeply and slowly open your eyes. Now ask yourself which Pond of Awareness scenario you want to create in your life for your children, yourself, and those around you ... and beyond.

## *Awareness* in Action

Without *awareness*, the tendency is to get caught up in your *subconscious fear*-based conditioning. Without *awareness*, nothing changes. But the good news is that *awareness* is a personal, conscious choice.

Being reactive or responsive is now a conscious choice. Hopefully having at least a slightly more enhanced level of *awareness*, which of the two pond scenarios do you intentionally choose to create from this point forward? Reflect on how your reactive anger-fueled behavior energetically charges the *Ripple Effect of Awareness* you generate and its impact on the people in your life, especially your children.

If you find yourself steaming because you are out to "get" your ex, then realize your anger is in control of you; you are not in control of yourself. Think about the emotional and psychological impact of your words and behavior on your children and what you are teaching them. Also realize that anger propagates stress for you and everyone your undermining energy touches. Knowing that stress is the greatest cause of illness and disease, why would you intentionally choose to go this route if you can choose the path of *split harmony*?

The realization of how much fear motivated my daily decision-making changed my life. Understanding the ways fear had been conditioned in my subconscious, particularly during my childhood from my father and mother, boggled my mind. I also realized how reactive I'd been during relationships with past girlfriends, my ex-wife, friends, and other personal relationships. *Awareness* offered me that valuable insight.

It took a 100 percent conscious commitment to be more *aware* of my choices, words, and actions, and to strive to make sure the consequences would be more positive for my daughter and for me. This was truly a life-changing *awareness* shift, one that to this day leads me to be more *responsible* for my choices.

You might not always be able to change or get rid of a specific fear, but by having *clarity* for the desired outcome and being *aware* in the moment, you can make empowered choices leading to more beneficial outcomes. As a parent of divorce, what could be more important for your children, who are going through their own duress during this challenging experience?

Yes, you can change the outcome of a situation or interaction when you change what used to be a conditioned, reactive habit. As you step into understanding the *Ripple Effect of Awareness* about how your choices impact others and learn to remain calmly responsive, others will no longer receive the subconscious reactions from you they expect.

*Awareness* is the third step in the process of truly manifesting *split harmony* in your life. As you become more *aware*, you can better execute a thoughtful and loving plan to ensure a difficult time for you and your ex doesn't have lasting effects on your children.

### • Reflective Questions •

*Write down your responses and thoughts for the greatest insight.*
*Do the work, experience the growth, and create* split harmony.

- What does *awareness* mean to you?
- How can you develop heightened *awareness* of yourself?
- How can you develop heightened *awareness* for how your choices impact the people in your life?
- How can you developing *awareness* really make a difference for your children?
- What can you do to be more open to self-growth, and why would you do so?

## STEP 4: THE *RIPPLE EFFECT OF AWARENESS*

- How can you find the people, mentors, and resources to provide insights and guidance to really help you learn and grow?
- What will it take for you to recognize the impact reacting to your *subconscious fears* is having on your children and on your relationship with them?
- What *subconscious fear* triggers you the most? (What pushes your anger button the easiest and most often?)
- What can you do to STOP reacting to your fears and become more *aware* and *responsible* for the example you are setting for your children?
- What is the *ripple effect* you want to create and be known for?

# CHAPTER 16

## STEP 5: TAKING PERSONAL *RESPONSIBILITY*

In many ways, the first three steps to securing *split harmony* simply work to shift our thoughts and behaviors to take personal *responsibility* for how our words, choices, actions, inactions, reactions, and the consequences of each, affect the people around us, especially our children. This truly begins and ends with the person you see in the mirror each and every morning. Stop to reflect on the impact of taking *responsibility* for your own integrity in your marriage/relationship. What would this look like and feel like? For you? For your kids? For your ex? From personal experience, I can tell you this creates a monumental shift in the health and prosperity of this crucial relationship.

Thanks to my mentor, Gretchen Pickeral, I woke up and realized I had to take personal *responsibility* for my words, choices, and actions to keep my daughter "out of the middle" of our divorce situation. I understood that every time a parents says, implies, or does something negative in reference to the other parent, children are immediately put "*in the middle*" from a psychological and emotional standpoint.

Children love their parents and do not care about the lack of trust, disagreements, blame, accusations, or any of the myriad of reasons behind the scenes causing the heated interactions leading to their parents' divorce. When parents develop the *awareness* it takes to stop blaming each other and start taking personal *responsibility* for their own behavior, it directly and positively impacts their children.

I have often wondered why so many parents of divorce seem to be oblivious about the ways they put their children *in the middle* as a direct result of their explosive, accusatory, defensive words and behavior. Children are often afraid to talk with one or both of their parents because of the scathing anger that exists between them. I believe it is each and every parent's personal *responsibility* to nurture and grow the foundation for honest and comfortable two-way-street communication with their children. When parents are reactive, kids will tend to shut down because they are afraid of what their parents' reaction will be toward them.

By working on improving your level of *responsibility*, you can take a moment to think before speaking, especially during those times when you feel the underlying anger surging to the surface. With practice, you can make more conscious and, subsequently, more positive choices regarding words spoken and actions that follow.

Remaining calm and being conscious promotes the ability to focus on handling any particular situation intentionally and in a nonreactive and more balanced mode. This is a gift to your children and reduces stress levels for everyone involved.

Whenever you as a parent (whether married, separated, or divorced) get blatantly angry at your ex, particularly over issues involving your children, have you ever stopped to consciously think about the impact your behavior has or will have on your children? (To clarify, this means *YOUR* behavior, NOT your partner's).

For most parents, the prevalent answer is no. Without even realizing it, parents of divorce tend to put themselves first because of their angst and do not consider the greater priority of their children.

Unfortunately, the all-too-typical reactive behavior of most parents of divorce is blatantly demonstrated by their immediate defensiveness. Each claims they are putting the children first, insists

## STEP 5: TAKING PERSONAL *RESPONSIBILITY*

they are right, and blames the other parent for whatever is wrong. Are you blaming your ex, thinking you are protecting your kids from him or her? Take a big breath, exhale, and ask yourself if this is something you do on a regular basis. Be honest.

This is a recipe for disaster and only serves to foster more retaliatory anger that can build into a blazing inferno of constant reactionary behavior. This further serves to plant subconscious seeds that can cause potential emotional and psychological upheaval for your kids. Unless one, or ideally both, of you recognize your own *responsibility* for the inflammatory situation you find yourselves in, your children will become more deeply embroiled in the midst of the flames.

The most unrecognized yet critical impact of almost every negative interaction between parents of divorce is that you end up putting your children *in the middle*. Period.

At times this may be the result of conscious behavior on the part of one parent or both parents. Know that this is one of the worst possible parenting scenarios. But it is avoidable. Ultimately you can take *responsibility* and change the narrative. If your ex won't step up, then commit to take personal responsibility on your end to shift the dynamics.

### Nurturing *Split Harmony* by Taking *Responsibility*

To clarify what it means to nurture *split harmony*, let me ask you some direct questions. Do you want to set examples for your children via your behavior that teaches them to:

- Maintain self-control or allow someone else to push their buttons?
- Be reactive to their *subconscious fears* or be able to make conscious choices?
- Develop solid, integrity-based core ethics and morals or continually react and make poor choices with directly

correlated outcomes and consequences that impact their lives in unwanted ways?
- Honestly express and communicate with others or constantly react with frustration, resentment, and anger?
- Feel secure and comfortable or feel like they need to "walk on eggshells"?
- Truly listen or be more intent on responding, making others feel alienated?
- Be present and *aware* about how their words, choices, actions, and the resulting consequences impact themselves and those around them?
- Live a purposeful life filled with passion and excitement, setting goals and taking action to achieve them or end up an unmotivated underachiever?

Whether you realize it or not, your conscious and subconscious behavior impacts and conditions your children. A lack of *responsibility* is usually the unintended consequence of powerful conditioning.

How often do you catch yourself doing or saying something to your children that in hindsight reminds you of something your parents did that you didn't like?

Remember how unreasonable you thought your parents' behavior was and how it drove you absolutely nuts?

Here are some additional questions. I highly recommend writing down your answers:

- Was your mother or father defensive? Are you?
- Did you mother or father correct you all the time? Do you habitually do this with your children?
- Did your parents yell at you constantly? Do you yell at your kids?
- Did your parents try to control you? Were they overly

## STEP 5: TAKING PERSONAL *RESPONSIBILITY*

protective? How about you? Do you try to control your kids? Are you overly protective?
- Did your parents tell you how proud they were of you? Do you let your kids know how proud you are of them? Do you check in with your kids to see if they are proud of themselves?
- Did your parents consistently listen when you had something you really wanted or needed to tell them? Do you listen to your kids when they really need you to, no matter what the situation?
- If your children are old enough to talk, do you ever ask them what they want or need?
- Can you see the impact of your behavior on your children, especially in inflammatory situations? Is it possible that your anger gets in the way and has shut down your *awareness* in a manner that subconsciously leads to you make everything about yourself and blame your ex for the challenges the two of you are having?
- What type of example are you setting and what are the values you are instilling in your children?
- Being truly objective, what type of example is the other parent setting for your children?
- Together, what core values are the two of you instilling in your kids?
- Are you blaming your ex? If yes, how are YOU avoiding taking personal *responsibility* for YOUR choices and behavior?
- Can you imagine the internal emotional dilemma potentially being created within children when both parents are completely unaware of the examples they are setting?
- Do you think most separated and divorced parents give much thought to the traumatic emotional conditioning their

mutual behavior is causing in the psyche of their children?
- Have you ever reflected on this?

In answering these questions, you begin to take the first and very important steps toward shifting to a place of personal *responsibility*. When you have the sincere goal to put your children first, it's vitally important to be honest with yourself and have integrity.

A lot of divorced parents want their children to choose them over the other parent. This is one of the absolute worst things any parent can do and the fastest way to put a child immediately and directly *in the middle*.

To make matters even worse, this self-centered, typically anger-filled behavior can plant seeds of permanent resentment in your children.

This seems downright heinous, yet divorced parents do this regularly and will often go to extremes to one-up or outdo the other parent to make the children "choose them."

When one parent bad-mouths the other, it is the complete opposite of taking personal *responsibility*. Rather, this accusatory, resentment-fueled behavior is in the "blame, shame, and excuse-making" scapegoat category. Yet this seems to be the modus operandi for so many divorces.

Even in the instances where one parent has done something "immoral," the children will still love them, no matter what the other parent says to them. Then there are scenarios where one parent wants something different and takes the other's actions personally. They set out to destroy the parent they claim to still love because they blame them for what's happened, taking ZERO *responsibility* for their own choices that led to the situation in the first place.

With this in mind, why would anyone, including an "affected" parent, try to paint a picture portraying the other parent as bad or evil?

Since your children's characteristics and behavior, to a large

## STEP 5: TAKING PERSONAL *RESPONSIBILITY*

extent, are formed and molded from the examples of your behavior as a parent—conscious or subconscious, rational or irrational, calm or angry, loving or filled with spite and hate—it is vital to have *awareness* and to make taking personal *responsibility* an absolute top priority.

Commit to take personal *responsibility* for how you parent your children. By your consistent example, be dedicated to instilling solid core values in your children for their underlying thought processes, communications, and decision-making skills. Be an ethically, morally, rationally, nonreactive, and calm parent of divorce who lives by integrity-based principles, NOT by your angst. This is an essential key to nurturing well-rounded, balanced, *aware* children of divorce.

What your children see and experience from you is typically what you get back from them. Yes, they become very much like you, especially the parts of yourself you do not like. Most parents of divorce do not seem to be *aware* of the subconscious characteristics and fears they are passing on to their offspring.

I don't know about you, but when I began to recognize the times I was reacting to my ex-wife with frustration, anger, and resentment and interacting with my daughter in the same ways my parents used to deal with me, I couldn't believe it! It was a real eye-, heart-, and soul-opener!

Committing to be the best you and the best parent you can be takes *COURAGE*. To follow through, you must stop blaming the other parent and be 100 percent committed to BEING *responsible* for your words, choices, actions, inactions, reactions, and the consequences of each.

### • Reflective Questions •

*Write down your responses and thoughts for the greatest insight. Do the work, experience the growth, and create* split harmony.

- What does personal *responsibility* mean to you?

- When you blame your ex/ex-to-be for the hardships, challenges, and disagreements between the two of you, how does this impact your children?
- What behavior do you inadvertently exhibit that puts your children in the middle? Be aware that it's likely to be occurring somewhere, somehow.
- How can you start taking *responsibility* to improve or change your behavior to ensure you do not put your kids in the middle?
- What can you do to provide some balance when the other parent puts your children in the middle and refuses to take any personal *responsibility*?
- How can you attempt to speak with your ex in a calm, nonreactive manner to start reducing the angst between you and bring more balance to your family for the sake of your kids?
- What would it take from you to make this a possibility for your ex?
- What would it take from your ex to make this a possibility for you?

# SECTION IV

## MAKING *SPLIT HARMONY* A REALITY

Now that we've covered *forgiveness*, *clarity*, *awareness*, and *responsibility*, let's review a few other helpful approaches and concepts to support these fundamental steps. Learning to compromise and striving to be your best during the all-too-intense duress that comes with divorce is critical. As you continue on this journey, I hope you will feel inspired to commit to create and nurture *split harmony* in your former family unit, particularly for the sake of your children.

## CHAPTER 17

## THE BENEFITS OF COMPROMISE

Up to this point, we have discussed the four steps to nurture *split harmony*. These include 1) *forgiveness*, 2) *clarity of destination*, 3) *awareness*, and 4) taking personal *responsibility*. Each of these crucial concepts will help move you from the chaos of divorce and one step closer to the promised land of compassion. When two people can learn to compromise, it's all about giving a little to gain a lot. Your small sacrifice often ends up creating a prosperous and nurturing environment for your children, which is the ultimate goal of this book.

Compromise seems like such a simple concept. We do it every day in traffic, while waiting in line, with our friends, and in our professional responsibilities. Without compromise, there is often seemingly endless chaos. Yet in the stormy waters of divorce, compromise is tremendously challenging for most couples. In most divorce situations, compromise is a rare commodity. Remember, getting your way is not all that important in the grand scheme of things. Rather, your focus needs to be on working with your ex to reach compromises that will benefit your kids.

You have likely lost the trust you once had in each other and subsequently think your ex is out to get you, to get even, or that he or she is trying to control you or hurt you. It may be that the two of you are reacting with anger toward each other.

Think about the internal stress you create for everyone from the combative behavior between you. It is not good or healthy for anyone involved!

**Compromise Leads to Synergistic Growth**

Idealistically, it takes two to be a synergistic parental team in raising children, whether happily married, separated, or divorced. You simply cannot survive a separation without some sense of compromise. When this is impossible due to your ex (or maybe it's you!) donning the proverbial boxing gloves at every opportunity, your decisions can either make things worse (usually subconscious decisions) or better (definitely conscious decisions).

I realized I could make things better and became committed to having the *awareness* it takes to do that. That started by no longer reacting to the once seemingly constant reactive behavior of my ex-wife. I stopped saying negative things about my child's mother in order to stop putting my daughter *in the middle*. I learned to let things go by not taking them personally. My ex's anger toward me was a result of her own *BS*, NOT mine. Most of the time, it doesn't matter if things go my way. The bottom line is that it is much more important to figure out what is best for Alie.

By looking at *how* I was communicating instead of focusing on what I wanted to say, I began to effectively improve my communication skills. That allowed me to set a much better example and have a positive impact on my daughter.

It all boils down to taking personal *responsibility*. This is absolutely essential. You can only do this for yourself. Realize that you cannot make your ex want to work with you for the benefit of your children. However, you can work on changing your own behavior, thereby setting a better example for your kids and having a more positive

## THE BENEFITS OF COMPROMISE

impact on everyone in the family. That's the beauty of compromise—it only takes one person to make a difference.

By consistently compromising, there will be a much better chance the two of you will work to figure out how to compromise for the sake of your children.

You do not have to like each other, but you it's important to try to respect the fact that your ex is the other parent of your children. Understand that what you say and do will impact your children, and be *aware* that, regardless of any negative influence on your part, they will very likely always love the other parent.

When your ex refuses to work with you for the benefit of your children, choose to have the most positive impact you can by remaining calm. Commit to not stooping to the same levels demonstrated by your ex's examples.

When I reflected on my own behavior, I recognized I had been reacting with anger to the seemingly endless unreasonableness of my ex-wife. I then consciously chose to handle things differently from that point forward. When I do not like how my ex is reactively dealing with me, why in the world would I want to come back at her with similar reactive, angry, defensive words and actions? I don't because I refuse to emulate behavior I do not agree with. I would much rather learn from her behavior how I do NOT want to be and treat her in the way I would want to be treated during any and all circumstances.

There are bound to be times when your ex/ex-to-be refuses to work with you. When this occurs, calmly take a stand and change your behavior accordingly. This is how I dealt with the schedule situation discussed previously, and the result was a much more balanced and beneficial outcome for Alie.

I consider myself to usually be reasonable (an observation generally held by others close to me as well), and I realize at times my ex-wife has tried to work with me in the best way she knows how. It seems these are the times when things are going her way in her life and she is more balanced and happy.

Being *aware* of at least a few of her fears has helped me recognize when she is being reasonable (even when at first I do not think this is the case) and when she is being unreasonable and reactive. This allows me to compromise so as to not push her buttons while working to diffuse the situation.

The more challenging aspect for me is to recognize when I am the one who has been unreasonable and reactive. When this is the case, I take a few deep breaths and apologize so I can get back into integrity (with myself and with her).

At times, it's been difficult to hold my tongue, not have a retort, or not say something negative to my ex or about my ex to my daughter. However, I know I am definitely up to the task of setting the best example for myself, for my daughter, and for my ex-wife. That really becomes the essence of compromise—putting yourself second to the desired result. When I find myself not quite living up to this ambition, I forgive myself, express my apologies to the necessary party, learn from my mistakes, and continue to make progress toward being *aware* and remaining calm at all times.

## Compromise Is Easy . . . Even If It Doesn't Seem That Way

Compromise is really a straightforward concept. When parents of divorce with extremely different viewpoints can emphasize the common priority of their children, they can put aside their differences and let go of anger. When this occurs, compromise becomes a fairly easily achievable reality.

When reactive anger keeps raising its ugly head, compromising can seem almost insurmountable. For a number of reasons, people don't compromise. But on most occasions, it is directly related to fearing that your kids will think the other parent is better than you or will want to spend more time with them. It can also be related to fear

# THE BENEFITS OF COMPROMISE

that your children love the other parent more, fear of being wrongly accused, blamed, or "attacked," fear of not getting what you want, and fear that the other parent wants to take your children away from you.

In more challenging separation or divorce situations, there is almost never any compromise. Often a mutually embroiled defensive stance exists, with both parents preparing for battle. This is the outcome of the extreme reactive modes on the part of each parent of divorce.

Each "side" is afraid of what the other will do. The once loving and open communication between lovebirds takes a 180-degree turn into a tit-for-tat offensive battlefield with each participant striving to one-up the other side to retaliate and get revenge (as a result of taking things personally). In these cases, each parent is exhibiting zero personal *responsibility*.

The underlying reality of this typical ongoing interaction is a complete and universal no-win scenario, whether it be subconscious or conscious. This holds true for everyone involved, especially for any and all children.

Let me ask a basic question regarding the situation with your ex: If you were not afraid, if you were not angry, how would you approach and deal with situations involving your children or your ex/ex-to-be? You'd compromise, right?

And now another question: Are you truly and honestly open-minded when it comes to reflecting on your own behavior? This may be **the** key for you from this moment forward. What is your role of *responsibility* for the nonstop warfare between the two of you?

Hopefully, reflecting on this will provide a true revelation for you. You may have just become a much better parent, ex/ex-to-be, and person. Do you realize how huge this is?

Meet the challenge. Be a bigger person. Recognize that your behavior is setting a poor example and affecting your children. You can then commit to work on being your best and being able to compromise. Over time, by transforming your behavior and setting a more positive, less reactive example, those you interact and deal with will tend to change how they interact with you.

## Compromise Is Challenging Yourself

Since the concept of compromise is so easy to understand, the real challenge is implementing it into your life. Here's a personal challenge: The next time you feel yourself beginning to get angry at your ex (or at anyone, for that matter), take several big, slow, deep breaths to get more oxygen into your system, rebalance, calm yourself, and regain your composure. Then figure out how you can compromise, think things through, and not be reactive, even if it means giving up something you thought you wanted.

One of the most significant realizations in life is that you can only be taken advantage of if you allow someone to do so. A huge aspect of this is your ATTITUDE, your mindset!

If something specific normally bothers you, try letting it go. That's right: just let it go. In that capacity you are compromising with yourself. It's easier than you think. If you don't like it when a certain individual gets their way, let it go. If you don't get what you want, let it go. Now you cannot be taken advantage of!

When you don't let something bother you, it becomes insignificant. Remember the saying, "Don't sweat the small stuff, and it's all small stuff"? Learn it and live it. You will find the outcomes to be significantly different than you had expected.

When you can learn to recondition yourself to think things through and make conscious choices in the spirit of compromise instead of reacting when you feel your fear or anger triggers being squeezed, stress will start to lessen and dissipate. You will get closer to being balanced. What a gift to yourself, your children, and the other parent! (Yes, it's okay to give gracefully to someone you may not even like ... though remember, you once loved them).

# THE BENEFITS OF COMPROMISE

## A World Filled with Compromise Is a Beautiful World

Can you imagine if your ex/ex-to-be began to compromise and work with you? How would you feel? Would your children be better off? Would you feel less combative and want to work with him or her even a little more? Think of the tremendous potential if you both inched closer toward the middle.

It sometimes seems easier to be involved in warfare than to take the initiative of being a peacemaker, as this goes against a lifetime of conditioning. The most significant aspect of constant warfare is the example it sets—the subconscious conditioning that results—for your children. You are setting them up. Decide that under NO circumstances do you want to consciously set up your children for future warfare in their relationships.

Really, what do you have to lose? If fighting and arguing are constant, why not try compromising? Begin with something simple. Take the first step.

What are you afraid of? That you won't get your way? That your ex will get his or her way? So what? Be the bigger person. Become *aware* of your fears and commit to letting them go so you can focus on what you really want for you and your children.

Find inner peace. Do your best to make peace with the other parent. Even if it's not accepted or doesn't work, at least you are making the effort, and more importantly, you'll be setting a wonderful example for your children (and for your ex/ex-to-be).

Peace or war? Which would you prefer for yourself, for your children, and for the world? For peace to occur when situations are volatile, someone must take the first step and attempt to compromise or choose to accept the situation and stop being combative in return.

We are all different. When you can agree that being different is okay, that it's okay to disagree, there can be peace. Just imagine the ramifications of this for your family! For yourself! For beyond your family! Be up to the challenge. Step up and set an example that has the potential to create what you want for your children and for yourself.

### • Reflective Questions •

*Write down your responses and thoughts for the greatest insight. Do the work, experience the growth, and create* split harmony.

- When separated or divorced parents attempt to work together from a true place of integrity and have their children's best interests at heart, compromise should be simple. Why does it seem to be so difficult for you and your ex to compromise most of the time?
- What can YOU do to make compromise happen?
- What can you do differently to get your ex/ex-to-be to work with you?
- If your ex is refusing to work with you or compromise, what can you do to set a different, more positive example for your children?
- What would it take for you to change how you have been dealing with your ex?
- Being calm and rational, how would you make decisions regarding your ex?
- Looking at the situation objectively, is your ex the one trying to work with you and you're the one being unreasonable?
- Can you admit when you've screwed up or when there's a better way of handling a situation?

# CHAPTER 18

## BE YOUR BEST SELF NO MATTER WHAT!

The crucial underlying principles you teach your children via your own example are essential to helping form the very foundational core of their character. These principles include morals, ethics, self-control, values, how to deal with and interact with others, *awareness* of self and of others, realizing and understanding fears, self-discipline, listening skills, communication, and so on. These are all vital for your children's bedrock *belief system*, the way they make choices and decisions, the way they react to situations, and the values they have for their relationships, their work ethic, and their future success. The list goes on.

To set the best example I can for my daughter, I realize I absolutely need to BE intentionally self-*aware* so I can stop being reactive and consistently be consciously proactive.

I want to make sure I am BEING my best so I can keep my child out of the middle of the emotional scenario between the two of us. This is the culmination of what I have intentionally attempted to share with you as we've delved into *forgiveness, clarity, awareness,* and personal *responsibility*. Children of divorce already have soaring emotions simply because their parents are not getting along; don't reinforce this by engaging in reactionary aggravation.

At times this may mean simply keeping your mouth shut. Other times it calls for an absolute commitment to try to compromise. Most of the time it really doesn't matter what the other person has said, so why make the situation worse by reacting with an anger-driven outburst? When I catch myself in a reactive situation, I use my *awareness trigger* (the little red flag) to remind me that I do not want to feel either the emotional, energetic drain or the adrenaline spike of anger. This is the time to take a few slow, deep breaths to calm down and focus on what I really want. This helps me immediately raise my level of *awareness* and reconsider what I was about to say. Then I consciously determine to express my feelings and thoughts in a positive fashion, possibly ask a clarifying question, or choose to not say anything at all.

When my ex and I disagree, I now understand that it is important for me to acknowledge her opinion and feelings. This does not mean I have to agree with her, give in, or change my opinion. One of the best responses to help keep things calm is to simply say, "Thanks for sharing." This shows I have listened to her and acknowledged what she has said. I do not have to say anything else in return.

At times, I initially believe I am setting a good example for Alie. In hindsight and after serious reflection, I may realize I was reacting and therefore subconsciously teaching and conditioning my daughter in the exact same negative manner I allowed to trigger me in the first place. Sometimes I can figure this out on my own. Other times, Alie will ask me a question or say something which makes the aha lightbulb turn on. I suddenly leap from the dark realm of my subconscious into a more reflective, conscious state and into the light!

Occasionally someone may point something out to me that puts a new perspective on my reactive behavior. Being committed to learn and grow from my own mistakes, I consciously and consistently work on being more *aware* and taking more *responsibility* so I can transform and be more proactive moving forward.

Once in a while, I feel it is appropriate to share my feelings with Alie or ask a question to help teach her that it's okay to make mistakes, especially when we can learn so much from them. With true self-*awareness* you can learn from your own blunders or the mistakes of others and expand your *responsibility* horizon.

More times than I care to admit, I have realized in hindsight that the example I was setting was not what I would ever consciously intend. These moments certainly do not make me proud. However, these self-reflections have helped me realize I need to commit to a more consistently enhanced level of *awareness*.

I believe I have finally learned how to remain calm (well, at least most of the time) during situations with my ex-wife, whereas I used to be reactively explosive. Yes, she really knows how to push my buttons, but the bottom line is that I subconsciously allowed her to push them and reacted just the way she had come to expect!

Remaining calm leads to a more positive outcome for everyone involved, especially for Alie, yet also for me. I strive to teach Alie that when things come to a seeming impasse (such as the schedule debacle shared earlier), these are the moments when it is most important to remain consciously calm so you can avoid igniting yet another battle.

I regularly demonstrate that it is okay to be flexible when the other parent makes requests, and I have consistently done so much more readily than Alie's mom, who I think continues to be more reactive. This makes sense as I have been committed to working on myself. Of course, this is simply my observational opinion.

When Alie tells me about something her mom has done that she doesn't like, we typically discuss the different examples being set for her, what the choices are, how she can shift her own perspective to not take it personally, and how she can make her own choices in the future. During these discussions, I aim to not react and say something negative about her mom, which would be the easy way out. Ahh, discipline to follow through on my commitment is so crucial!

I have shown Alie that it is okay to have different ways of doing things, that people are unique and have dissimilar ways of dealing with life, both from the standpoint of a daily routine and for the longer term. For example, when we travel, I have Alie call her mom just about every day, which is something that is rarely reciprocated. When Alie is with her mom, her mom does not seem to like it when Alie wants to call me.

Why do I do all of this? It is certainly not to win a popularity contest. I do this because I recognize wholeheartedly that I have a *responsibility* as a parent to be the best parent I can be, especially when times are tough or seem utterly impossible. I don't have the luxury of just saying or doing whatever I want. I have an example to set for my daughter and therefore strive to be the best version of myself I can be. Not for me—for Alie.

Here are some of the most significant *awareness* points and characteristics that have helped me follow through on being the best version of myself:

**Parental Conditioning.** I believe the most negative examples I've set for my daughter are times I have subconsciously repeated the parental conditioning I experienced in my childhood. I recognize that I've tended to be defensive, so I have been working diligently on having the *awareness* to release this reactive, disempowering trait. I do not want to condition Alie to develop the same oblivious habit.

**Filtering.** At times, I treated Alie more like an adult than a child. I shared too much information or went too in-depth expressing my feelings about her mother and the details of how her mother dealt with a specific circumstance, including when I thought her mom was being too critical. The irony here: I was doing exactly what I was complaining about and being judgmental and critical of her mom. How many times have you been cynically two-faced?

**Listening.** One of the single most important examples I can set for my child is to truly listen (without interrupting when I have the intent to share my two cents). This includes listening to my ex-wife when she is calm. When she is upset and yelling, I can calmly set boundaries and let her know we can talk and I will listen when she calms down. True listening is consciously paying attention so you can really hear what the other person is saying and understanding any unspoken underlying meaning. Asking clarifying questions is an excellent way to make sure you are respectfully hearing what is being said. There may be times (especially during the teenage years) when true listening can be very challenging. During these potentially demanding moments, it may be most effective to simply listen and hold your tongue instead of speaking your mind. When reacting to your triggered fears and emotions, most of the time you will only create additional anguish and disrespect. Pay attention if you find yourself thinking that you are the one who deserves the respect from your kids. Respect is a two-way street!

**Communicating Effectively.** Your children begin to learn communications skills as infants. One of the most significant ways they learn is through observing how you listen (or don't listen) to others. As they grow older, listening becomes more important and is an integral component of child/parent relationships. It takes *clarity, awareness,* and *responsibility* to set the best example for your children. Effective, people-centric communication skills lie at the most basic core of nurturing lifetime, bonding relationships with your children, your soul mate, your friends, and your colleagues. If you do not (or cannot for lack of *clarity, awareness,* and *responsibility*) listen to your own children, you may never really get to know them, earn their two-way respect, or build a truly meaningful, open, and honest communication-based bond.

**Being *Aware*.** When you think it's vital to speak your mind, having the level of *awareness* to make sure you can do so with loving intent is key if you want your children to listen to you in return. Remember, you are the one setting the example! Maybe you're like me. One of my greatest desires as a parent has been to nurture and build a relationship with my daughter where we can consistently have open and honest discussions. She is now a young adult, and this has become an incredible reality. The seeds for this were planted during her early childhood, and I continue to strive to be *aware* so I can water them.

## Fear Challenges Being the Best Version of Yourself

Think about the following two questions very carefully and and answer them with consummate honesty: 1) *How do I want to impact my children?* and 2) *What do I want to teach them?*

I've grown to the point where I am *aware* of the examples I set for my daughter, and I am committed to making more conscious choices and decisions, especially regarding interactions with her mom.

I have also become more perceptive of others and am continually learning from their words, actions, reactions, and behavior. This helps me glean more *clarity* for what I want to emulate and what I want to make sure I do NOT repeat under any circumstances.

You can learn so much by revisiting and reflecting on how you have handled situations. Subsequently you will begin to make more *aware* and conscious decisions about how you want to deal with similar situations in the future.

One of the best ways to set a consistently positive example for your children: Remain calm no matter what the situation. Remember, when your anger surfaces and causes you to react, you have lost control.

For example, my daughter's mother would tell her that her hair looked terrible whenever she was with me. (Realize I am simply sharing an example, not berating my ex). When Alie was nine she did her own hair when she was with me. Her mom did Alie's hair when they were together. My ex-wife was making a direct criticism of her own daughter, not of me. How do you think this might have affected or conditioned our daughter and her self-confidence? This is a significant instance of how anger can blind you to the way your words and actions impact your children.

It can be quite challenging to bite your tongue and not say the first thing that pops into your head. When you spew forth, you are no longer in control. And you will probably instill more resentment in your ex/ex-to-be.

You may not know how things are done in the home of the other parent when your children are with them. Jumping to conclusions and reacting with negative, assumptive outbursts can be a direct criticism of your children, not of the other parent.

In any given moment, you can teach, influence, and condition your children. Do you want to influence your kids to repeat your out-of-control flare-ups, or do you want to help them become *aware* and teach them compassion and acceptance?

When you develop a higher level of self-*awareness*, you can begin to recondition yourself to stop, consciously think, and then respond or act (versus reacting immediately because of your fears). When you have mastered this "skill set" to be at the core of all your interactions with your children and your ex/ex-to-be, you will be setting an inspirational example. And more than likely you will start to notice a significant difference in the outcomes of interactions with your ex.

When someone is so self-consumed by their own deeply rooted anger, they become oblivious of others, including their own children. Their vision of reality becomes clouded with resentment and anger. As a result, they cannot operate from a place of love and compassion.

Such individuals are unable to accept and forgive. They end up teaching anger, hatred, and fear to their own children through their own behavior and the examples it sets. They tend to blame and shame their ex and make up excuses to rationalize their own behavior.

Is this even remotely close to what you're doing? Are these the type of things you want to teach your children?

Without being *aware* of your fears and how they control you, they can strip you of your potential happiness. You may often attempt to rationalize your behavior by interpreting your reactions of anger and fear as self-preservation or protecting the kids. The irony is that in reality you are possibly hurting everyone involved. The most affected "victims" are usually your children.

Though you may not realize it, you also affect yourself and the other parent. When you or the other parent step into a new relationship, you often affect these individuals as well through your continued subconscious reactiveness to your fears. Everyone loses! This is indeed a setup for the *Vicious Cycle of Subconscious Fear*. The tragic irony: this puts out resistance to what you really want (assuming you have *clarity* for what you want for your children and for yourself).

With this profound insight, you can move forward by choosing to follow through on setting the best example you can for your children. In other words, resolutely commit to consistently being your best self. This can be quite challenging, especially during extreme times of duress. Being *aware* of the difference this will make for you and your children will allow you to focus and stay on track. By knowing with *clarity* the values you want to instill in your kids, you can move forward with the passion and desire necessary to follow through on this altruistic goal.

The rewards will come as your kids grow older, as they learn one way or the other from you consistently setting a positive example. If you have an ex/ex-to-be who works with you, is calm, and has the ability to communicate and compromise, be eternally grateful. Simply express your gratitude to them.

### Real-Life Success Stories

I've heard story after story of truly caring and remarkable parents navigating divorce in a respectful and caring manner. They make their kids the top priority, and their actions constantly reflect this focus. Here are a few positive and mutually empowering examples of how parents of divorce can work together for the sake of their children and for themselves:

An ex-husband called his ex-wife to discuss a new church he wanted to take their children to on a Sunday morning. He wanted to make sure she did not have any issues with the kids going to a new church. She didn't—and she was grateful that he was considerate and respectful of her opinion.

This is a simple yet wonderful example of how two-way, mutual respect can lead to being appreciative of your ex-spouse. Just think of how wonderful it is for children of divorce to have parents demonstrate mutual respect to and for each other!

The same couple apparently has a similar philosophy regarding their interactions with each other for anything concerning their children. They will do whatever it takes to make things go smoothly. Even when they disagree, they each accept that the other parent has good and honorable parenting intentions.

During a phone conversation to go over the next year's schedule, they took less than two minutes to figure out a custody arrangement for the entire year. This is quite an exemplary display of respect—and what a wonderful example to set for their children!

Another example is a story I heard of one parent who traveled a lot for business and the other parent was open, flexible, and willing to work regarding the scheduling for the children. There was no tit for tat such as insisting to make up for lost days. When the traveling parent requested a change, even last minute, the other one readily compromised and easily and agreeably made adjustments to the schedule so the kids could see the traveling parent when they returned home.

This sets a great example for the kids. Compromise. Working together. Being reasonable. Less stress and higher levels of peace and happiness are the result for all. It is categorically sad that the majority of separated and divorced parents do not have this type of attitude and outlook.

It is a wonderful feeling to acknowledge and express gratitude to your ex/ex-to-be for the positive way they interact with you in raising and setting a good example for your precious children.

To those parents who commit and put forth the effort to work together, I commend you and say, "Congratulations for having the *COURAGE* to *forgive*, the mutual commitment to glean *clarity* for what you want for your children, the desire to develop heightened *awareness*, and the integrity and fortitude to start taking personal *responsibility* to follow through in order to create and nurture *split harmony*."

### • Reflective Questions •

*Write down your responses and thoughts for the greatest insight.*
*Do the work, experience the growth, and create* split harmony.

- How much anger and resentment do you feel toward your ex/ex-to-be?
- How is your angst causing you to be defensive and reactive?
- How can you start setting a more positive example for your children?
- What are the ways you are positively teaching your children through the examples you set?
- What are the ways you are negatively teaching your children through your reactiveness?
- What is one thing you can do differently to create a positive shift in your divorce relationship scenario?
- What values are important to you? What values do you want to teach your children? How do you intend to do this?

# CHAPTER 19

## CREATING AND NURTURING *SPLIT HARMONY*: *FORGIVENESS + CLARITY + AWARENESS + RESPONSIBILITY = SPLIT HARMONY*

Fortunately, I've had a few dear friends who could tell it to me "like it is." Our friendship is based on openness, honesty, and integrity, so the communication between us has always been direct. At times, they pointed out circumstances with my ex-wife and her behavior and my behavior that were not necessarily as black-and-white as I had originally thought. If I overreacted, I heard about it from my true friends. As a result, I could focus on learning life-changing lessons from my own reactive conduct and shift my perspective and subsequently my behavior. This has been an absolute gift, especially for Alie, yet also for me. There is no doubt in my mind that this learned ability has helped me create and nurture *split harmony*.

In today's world it appears that blaming, shaming, and excuse-making have taken over. Parents of divorce rarely exhibit personal *responsibility*. STOP blaming your ex (or someone else) and look in the mirror. There you will see the cause of your challenges and, more importantly, the solution. Take a huge, calming breath and reflect on how you can create *split harmony* for your children (and beyond your family) by having *forgiveness* in your heart, *clarity* for what you want to create for your children, *awareness* of the impact of your words, choices, actions, reactions, and inactions, and taking personal *responsibility* for your choices and subsequent behavior and for the *ripple effect* you have spawned.

If you are in the midst of an unpleasant or dreadful divorce scenario, you may be thinking it is impossible to create, much less nurture, an environment of *split harmony* for your former family unit. You may be thinking there is no way you are doing anything positive for that son-of-a-bitch former husband or bitch former wife. I was there once, and I get it. It's their fault, and you'll do anything to make sure they're miserable.

If you find yourself agreeing at any level that this is where you are, it's a wake-up call to start making a positive shift. Your own stress, sense of well-being, balance, and happiness should be enough to inspire you to "wake up and smell the coffee."

If you've gotten anything out of what you've read so far, and if you've done any of the work within these very pages, I pray you've had at least a spark of hope ignited. You don't know what you don't know, and now you've had a pretty good dose of insights and lessons concerning the realm of divorce. We've all been conditioned since childhood, and until you have an eye-opening dose of *awareness*, nothing is likely to change and the habitual reactions will continue.

In the battleground of your disintegrating marriage, to have any environment of *split harmony*, you must try to let go of your angst. The first step is to forgive yourself and then to at least have the desire to forgive your ex-to-be. If you don't think this is possible, it's a sign that this is truly the first step.

Anger and resentment do not serve any positive purpose in the realm of divorce for you, for your kids, or for anyone in your entire former family unit. It causes stress and creates more stress, anger, and resentment for you and your ex/ex-to-be. The tragedy is that it teaches these very things to your children via the example you and your ex are living and breathing each and every day.

## CREATING AND NURTURING *SPLIT HARMONY*

Make the conscious decision to shift and find *forgiveness* in your heart, at the very least for yourself. You were once in love with the very person you are now battling, so find in it in your heart to try to forgive them. This does not mean you have to agree with, be with, or be in love again with him or her. It does not mean you have to accept unreasonable accusations or behavior. The purpose is to replace your fear, angst, and resentment with *forgiveness*. Ultimately, your ex might be willing to forgive you in return. If not, it's okay; at the very least you will be helping and empowering yourself and your children. It takes two to tango, but it only takes one to make a difference. Commit to your children and to yourself that you will make positive changes, because it's up to YOU to make **the** difference. This is a life-changing and important goal for you and especially for your children. This is a perfect time to take one more look at the fundamental steps for creating and nurturing *split harmony*.

### Step 1: *Forgiveness*

*Darkness cannot drive out darkness; only light can do that.*
*Hate cannot drive out hate; only love can do that.*
—Martin Luther King Jr.

*Forgiveness* cleans the slate so you can glean *Clarity*, have heightened *Awareness*, and start taking personal *Responsibility* for your behavior so you can create and nurture *split harmony* for yourself, for your children, and for the entire former family unit. Radiate *split harmony* and receive more *harmony* in return.

### Step 2: *Clarity* of Your Destination

*I can't change the direction of the wind,*
*but I can adjust my sails to always reach my destination.*
—Jimmy Dean

To reach your destination, you first have to know where you want to go. This is what the *COURAGE* principle, *Clarity of Destination*, is all about.

To figure out what you want as far as the environment of divorce goes, ask yourself, *What do I really want?* When you have progeny, it's vital to ask, *What do I want for my children and is my behavior creating it for them?*

When your fear, angst, or resentment leads you to spew outbursts of blame, shame, and excuses for your behavior, understand that you are putting out immense resistance to whatever it is you really want for your children.

Know what you want to create, and commit to being the person it takes to create it. If what you want stems from your frustration, anger, and bitterness toward your ex/ex-to-be, realize that any *clarity* is completely lost in the murkiness of your dark fears and reactive, emotion-fired thoughts and behavior. Know that if you are in a retaliatory, spiteful revenge mode, it can be extremely destructive and harmful for your kids, for yourself, and yes, for your ex.

What if you and your ex forgive and let go of the angst and resentment that has the two of you embroiled in an exhausting, seemingly never-ending battle over your kids, custody, finances, home, and so much more? Imagine if you could put your kids first and reduce the disagreements, constant arguing, and embattlement. The outcome would be reduced stress, saved financial expenditures for divorce attorneys (meaning more for each of you, your children, or the philanthropic causes close to your heart), and inherent turmoil being replaced with inner peace.

*Forgiveness* and *Clarity* are imperative to creating this miraculous, though very realistic, scenario. The choice is up to you.

## Step 3: *Awareness*

> *What is necessary to change a person is*
> *to change his awareness of himself.*
> —Abraham Maslow

Nothing inside of you can shift until you have the *awareness* that things aren't the way you want them to be. Gain *Clarity* for what you DO want, and then realize that something has to change—and this change is up to you, and only you. *Awareness* about your thoughts, words, choices, actions, reactions, inactions, and the consequences of each is how you can begin to create a shift inside of you, for who you are and how you are intentionally being.

The *Ripple Effect of Awareness* is all about being conscious enough to realize how your words, choices, actions, reactions, inactions, and the corresponding ripples of each impact the people in your family and your life.

When you constantly admonish and demean others or rationalize your own behavior, you are at your worst. To change these negative examples you've been setting for your children, first perceive how you've been habitually conditioned to be reactive and point fingers at others, especially at your ex during the emotional forbearance of the annulment of your marriage. Use *Awareness* to shift from being a reactive cog in the wheel into being your best, most authentic self and an integrity-charged champion for your children.

## Step 4: Personal *Responsibility*

> *You must take personal responsibility. You cannot change the circumstances, the seasons, or the wind, but you can change yourself. That is something you have charge of.*
> —Jim Rohn

# SPLIT HARMONY

*Awareness* is where it all begins, yet personal *responsibility* is where the real empowerment occurs. Without being *responsible* for your thoughts, words, choices, actions, reactions, inactions, and the consequences of each, nothing will ever change.

In the world of divorce, and in all areas of life, one of the major direct causes for most problems and challenges is that people are devoid of *responsibility*. Our universe is full of blamers, shamers, and excuse-makers. When you blame your ex, or anyone else, it tends to ignite a defensive response, and the blame gets deflected right back at you.

When you shame your ex (or someone else), people think you are showing what you're really made of: a belittling, self-centered, egotistical, obnoxious, ungrateful know-it-all. When you make up excuses for something you said or did, you are being spineless and completely irresponsible. This may seem harsh, but be courageous and reflect on this for a few minutes.

Blaming, shaming, and excuse-making are all the absolute complete opposite of what it means to take *Responsibility* and to *Be Responsible*. Are any, much less all of these, what you really want to teach your children for their future? What you put out is what you get back, often in multitudes. Stop bitchin' and moanin' and step up to the plate for the choices you've made and those you'll make from this point forward. Shift the future possibilities for your children by shifting who you are. Start operating from a place of true, honest, heartfelt integrity so you can create and nurture *Split Harmony*.

Godspeed, and God bless your children.

*With Faith, COURAGE, Inspiration, Gratitude, and Love,*

*Peter Hobler*
*The "Ex-Factor"*
www.theex-factor.com

# POSTLUDE:

## FOUR STEPS TO BEGIN NURTURING *SPLIT HARMONY*:

1. Describe where you stand as far as being able to forgive yourself and your ex.
2. *Describe with clarity what you want to create for your children.*
3. *Describe your level of awareness regarding your thoughts, words, choices, actions, reactions, inactions, and the consequences of each.*
4. *How are you taking personal responsibility for your words, choices, actions, reactions, inactions, and the impact of each in your divorce scenario?*

# ABOUT THE AUTHOR

**Personal Purpose**
To Inspire More People Through
Active and Courageous Teaching

***Split Harmony* Mission**
To inspire parents to remove the angst from
separation and divorce for the sake of their children.

**Peter Hobler, MBA,** is the driving force behind "The Ex-Factor" brand, developer of The 7 Principles of COURAGE, architect of The Vicious Cycle of Subconscious Fear, author of *COURAGE to Find the FIRE Within: Invest in Yourself to Discover Your Passion*, personal development coach, and keynote speaker.

Peter is committed to continually learn from his past choices and mistakes and is passionate about working on himself and making a difference in the lives of others. Three of his greatest personal epiphanies are: 1) Everything you say and do as a parent sets an example for and impacts your children; 2) What you focus on is what you attract more of into your life ... so begin by gleaning true *Clarity* for what you want for your kids; and 3) Only one person is *Responsible* for your words, choices, actions, reactions, and the ripple effects of each ... the person in the mirror.

## BE SURE TO VISIT MY WEBSITE . . .
## AND A BONUS OFFER

Be sure to visit **www.splitharmony.com** for further insights and guidance, and to learn more about Peter and *The Ex-Factor*.

Plus, Peter is offering a free Bonus Offer for all readers of *Split Harmony*. Go to **www.splitharmony.com/quiz** to take a short quiz. After taking the quiz, you will receive insights regarding how you are impacting your kids and your overall divorce situation.

You can also sign up for Peter's newsletter at:
**www.splitharmony.com/newsletter**

www.ingramcontent.com/pod-product-compliance
Lightning Source LLC
Chambersburg PA
CBHW071734080526
44588CB00013B/2020